How to Use
The Science of Mind

How to Use
The Science of Mind

Ernest Holmes

Science of Mind Publishing
Golden, Colorado

CONTENTS

v

CONTENTS

FOREWORD

IT'S WITH A GREAT GRATITUDE THAT I WRITE THIS FOREWORD TO *How to Use the Science of Mind*. It gives me an opportunity to repay, just slightly, the huge debt I owe to Dr. Holmes and his teachings. I can honestly say I divide my life in terms of "Before Science of Mind" and "After Science of Mind." This sounds corny, but it's true. Don't get me wrong; I've had a great life. I grew up in a great small town and had a happy, relatively conventional childhood. I was outgoing and curious. I had opportunities to work and make extra money for all the things kids think they need. I had a great family and friends, and I felt connected with what I called God. However, I didn't go to church anymore because the God they preached just didn't match the God I knew. I also felt powerless to escape my life trajectory. Based on the cultural environment, I was destined to marry someone in the logging industry, stay home, have kids, and perhaps add income to the family as a clerk or in some other "womanly" profession. (My father, in all his paternal loving wisdom, wanted me to work for a government agency because it would offer the most security.)

My heart and soul, however, wanted none of the above. Then a friend introduced me to the works of Ernest Holmes and his textbook, *The Science of Mind*. That was the beginning of my new life. It didn't happen overnight, of course. In all honesty, for the longest time I just didn't "get" the guy, the ideas were so foreign to my mental constructs. But as I let the wisdom speak deep to my soul, my soul responded with "yea and Amen" (the head, or intellect is often the last to catch on).

So, After Science of Mind, I gave myself permission to look at jobs and careers that none of my peers were considering. I started to believe I could be successful—even very successful—financially; I let myself consider the vast fields of infinite possibilities. That was new. Then I used the techniques taught in this book to live those possibilities. I'm living a life I would have never considered possible Before Science of Mind. Now, I frequently ask myself, what's next?

So, dear reader, I can say with all conviction, this book could change your life (you've read that before I'm sure). The catch is you need to apply what you read. Don't wait to thoroughly understand Dr. Holmes' ideas of how it works, just start working it. Understanding will follow; in the meantime you could be living the life of your dreams.

—*Kathianne Lewis, D.D.*
Seattle, Washington

INTRODUCTION

THERE IS A POWER FOR GOOD IN THE UNIVERSE AVAILABLE TO everyone and you can use it.

This book teaches you what this Power is, how it works, and how you can use it to help yourself and others. If you will accept the simplicity of its statements and follow the instruction given in the examples of how to use this Power, you will find yourself engaged in the greatest experiment of your life.

The human mind needs, and must have, a direct approach to Spirit. It is natural for us to reach out from our ignorance to Its enlightenment, from our weakness to Its strength, from our darkness to Its light. Somewhere along the line we shall have to surrender our weakness to Its strength, our fear to Its faith, our lack to Its abundance.

This book teaches you how to pray scientifically. It is applied Christianity.

Faith not only lays hold of a power which actually exists, it causes this power to respond as though it were a law of good operating for you. Why shouldn't we have an unlimited faith in life? It had intelligence enough to make everything, including ourselves.

And now, because we need it so much, and because we feel we

can no longer live without it, we are going to act as though it were right here, always responding to us, loving us in spite of our mistakes.

The disciples of Jesus watched him in his ministry among the sick and among the multitudes who heard him so gladly. They had seen new light come into the eyes of those whose vision had been dulled. They had seen a new energy flowing through the limbs of those who had been paralyzed. They had seen the lame walk, the dumb speak and the deaf hear. And so they asked him to teach them how to pray.

The pages of this book are devoted to an explanation of his answer.

—*Ernest Holmes*

Ernest Holmes produced many of his writings early in the twentieth century and, following conventions of that era, often used generic masculine forms in referring to both men and women. Rather than alter this book to reflect contemporary usage, Science of Mind Publishing has, in most cases, retained his original style.

INDIVIDUALIZING
UNIVERSAL POWER

SPIRIT IS THE CREATIVE CAUSE BACK OF AND WITHIN EVERY-thing. God is not *a* spirit, but *the* Spirit. This one Spirit is the spirit of all people. A philosophy of unity permits many mentalities but only one Mind, innumerable individualized points in the creative consciousness of an Absolute which always remains one, undivided and indivisible unity.

It is because the Mind of God, which is the creative mind of the universe, flows through man that man's thought is creative. It is because of man's nature and not his will that his thought is creative. Who by taking thought—as though he were independent of the universal Mind to do anything—who "by taking thought" can change his spiritual nature or "add one cubit" to its stature?

Man has a mentality. He has *a* spirit in the sense that *the* Spirit is individualized through him, but his spirit is not separate from God, for God as man, in man, is man. Man is individual

1

while God is universal. The Universal individualizes Itself in the individual. "The highest God and the innermost God is one God." This One includes man.

Man is an individualized center of Divine Thought and through him the Original Thinker is finding a fresh starting point for Its creative power. Therefore, without violating universal or natural laws, the mind of man steps in to specialize or make personal use of them.

Man, then, is given power over his own life. He cannot alter the laws of nature, but he can so alter his relationship to them that that which had bound him may now free him. He has been given the prerogative of spontaneous thinking. He has been given the ability to initiate a new chain of causation. He announces his own activity. This activity is an activity of the Divine Mind operating through him. It is the original creative Cause doing something new through him.

There is but one Mind and we use It. The laws of nature are universal. Our use of them is individual and personal. This is the secret of spiritual mind practice. Our thought is operated on by a universal creativity which is infinite in its capacity to accomplish. Thus, in taking thought we do not force anything, we merely decide what thought to follow, knowing that the result is automatic.

This idea of the oneness of God is not a philosophy of absorption or annihilism. We do not become absorbed in the universal Self to the loss of individuality. Quite the opposite. We find ourselves, not absorbed, but immersed, in a Universality, each one being a unique, individual and different manifestation of that which itself is one, undivided, indivisible and whole.

We cannot think of the Spirit as static, but as forever unfolding Its divine nature. It is doing this in the physical universe independently of our personal thought. In our personal lives It

must do this through our thinking. In such degree as our thinking is in accord with the original Nature, the same orderly procession of harmonious ideas will operate in our affairs that is
already operating in that larger world which we experience but
neither create nor control. This leaves us individual freedom
within the law of universal harmony, individual will within a
universal coordinating will.

As all deep spiritual thinkers have announced, and rightly, we
soon come to realize that wherever the individual will is contrary
to, or in opposition to, this universal coordinating will, it detach-
es itself from the source of its power, it goes alone and soon
becomes exhausted. On the other hand, wherever the individual
will links itself up with the universal harmony, it becomes a
spontaneous proclamation of that harmony, now individualized.

In spiritual practice we follow the stream of the individual
life back to the original Source from which it emerged and in
which it still lives, moves and has its being. This is an important
part of our treatment, to connect the Universal with the individual, and the individual with the Universal.

Instead of denying that God is personal to each, we should
emphasize such personalness. It is one of the chief cornerstones
of this spiritual philosophy. Each individual life is a unique
expression of the universal Wholeness. No two lives can or
ought to be alike. The one universal Life flows through everything. We give individual expression to It.

Life can do for us only what It does through us. We are like
an artist who sets up his canvas on a shore, wishing to paint a
marine scene. Because he is an individual, he will interpret the
scene in the light of his own consciousness. He might think, "I
want seagulls in this picture. I want a boat in the distance. I want
children playing on the shore. And through it all I want a great
sense of peace, calm and beauty."

He is giving individual expression to this particular scene. He meditates on the beauty and the peace he wishes to portray and adds the personal thoughts that come to him. No other person ever did or ever can catch the same expression that he does on this particular canvas. It will be unique. He is not robbing God of His peace or beauty. He is merely expressing it as he experiences it within himself in relationship to this particular scene.

We are always specializing the Law of cause and effect for some purpose. Mostly we are doing this unconsciously. Now we must learn to bring our thoughts and purposes into line with the original harmony. In doing this we should not be afraid that we are usurping the Divine Will any more than a farmer would be afraid that he is going contrary to the laws of nature or the will of God when he decides to plant corn instead of cotton. The necessity of choosing is ordained by the very nature of our being, and we cannot escape it.

We are at liberty to choose what manner of life we shall live. We should feel that in this choice we are backed by all the will, all the purpose and all the law in the universe. Our reliance is on this law and order. It is the creative agency of all life and at the same time our use of it is personal and individual.

Here is all the freedom one could ask for and all the freedom that the Divine Mind itself could possibly have given us—the freedom to act as an individual, the freedom to give full rein to our creative imagination, the freedom to do this, at least temporarily, in such a way as to produce discord instead of harmony; and more important, the freedom to produce harmony instead of discord.

If we couple with this the idea that no one can harm another without ultimately hurting himself, that good alone can finally win, we shall see that when any individual's consciousness is in tune with the Infinite he need no longer ask, "Does God wish me to be happy or whole?" or, "Does the Law of Good desire me to have this thing which I desire?" He need merely ask, "Can I conceive of this as being done? Am I certain that my desire is in line with good? If it is, nothing is against me and everything is for me."

The Divine Mind does not necessarily contain a mental blueprint of everything the individual is going to do. It does, however, contain the possibility of all individual action. When anyone conceives a new idea, thinks up a new plan for procedure, which is in accord with the Divine Nature, then God Himself is going forth anew into creation through that individual. And that person may, and should, expect that all the power and all the presence there is will creatively flow through his individual word because he has complied with the fundamental law of harmony governing all life.

This should be particularly interesting to an inventor, an artist, a writer, or anyone who is introducing new ideas into the world. In actual practice he trains his mind to listen to the Divine Harmony. He affirms that this Divine Harmony is now operating through his own intelligence, governing it, directing it, stimulating it into action. He so formulates his thoughts and ideas that they will in no way detract from this Divine Harmony. He can test them easily enough by being certain that they are life-giving, that there is nothing in them that could rob or hurt anything that lives.

When we say there is one Cause back of all manifest form, one Intelligence back of all consciousness, and one Spirit within all men, we are not denying the reality of created forms or individual experience. We are affirming the unity of all life, a unity which includes all variety. Unity passes into variety and multiplicity without division. In each creation Life brings Its whole nature to bear upon that individual expression. Thus every man's life not only has God, but all of God, back of, within and through him.

The significance of this we but dimly perceive, yet, by some interior awareness which all people possess, we sense the Divine Presence and know that we are part of It. Everyone should feel in intimate relationship with the Spirit. This has been the essence and the vitality of all religious convictions throughout the ages. No matter how crude they may have been, they have been built on a solid, substantial, permanent and changeless Reality.

Everyone needs the warmth and color, the imagination and feeling of a sense of intimacy with the creative Spirit. Our intellect yearns toward It as naturally as a rose turns to the sun. In spiritual mind healing it is important that we sense an infinite Personalness back of, in and through everyone. Without this our work would have no warmth or color. It would be without feeling, therefore, unproductive, uncreative, dead.

Listening to the Divine Presence, desiring only that which is right, the practitioner of spiritual mind science must know that he is using a Law of cause and effect which is immutable. It knows how to do anything. It knows how to take his thoughts and ideas and actually project them into specific conditions. These conditions will automatically correspond to his mental acceptance, to his real, actual and embodied subjective acceptance and identification.

Man not only has a right to individualize creative power, nature has imposed this necessity upon him. He has no choice other than to use this creative power. His thought will always be creative, whether he knows it or not. The creativity of man's thought has nothing to do with his will or his belief; it is here just as nature is here. It is the *use* of a creative power that man has control over, not the thing itself.

6

The conscious use of spiritual power is the finest of arts because it has deep feeling. It is the greatest of all intellectual perceptions because it is the most penetrating. It is religious in that its whole thought is based on the intimate relationship of the Spirit with everything that is. It is scientific in that it deals with law and order.

We should accept this proposition and see what we can do with it. Have we enough conviction to turn from negative conditions and mentally contemplate their opposites? Can we turn from poverty and want to the acceptance of abundance? Can we turn from sickness to a belief in health? Can we turn from unhappiness to happiness? Can we shut out discord long enough to contemplate harmony? And have we the courage to proceed on this basis?

The effective practitioner in this science has the will to try, the courage to make the attempt, the faith to believe in himself because he has confidence in the Law of Good. The simplicity of this conviction is enhanced when he realizes he has nothing to change outside himself.

LAW OF MIND IN ACTION

MIND TAKES FORM THROUGH THE LAW OF ITS OWN BEING. THIS is a law in nature, and, like all such laws, must be accepted. Unless one had a deep conviction that there is a principle of mind which operates from thought to thing, through a definite law, he would have no principle to demonstrate and no method to use.

We cannot separate thoughts from things and hope to demonstrate things through thinking. This is the most subtle thing about mental treatment. One must have a deep conviction that the word is operated on by a spiritual law. The practitioner works with ideas. He theoretically resolves things into thoughts and works in the realm of mind only, with no sense of personal responsibility, because the Law is the doer.

The practitioner makes his declarations and knows that a Power acts on them. He does not put the power into the Law. He takes it out. This spiritual realization now becomes law, acting independently of any existing circumstances, and being able to create new circumstances out of itself. This he must know.

The spiritual mind practitioner is in an identical position with any other person who uses a law of nature. Everyone expects to comply with laws if he hopes to use them. The Law of Mind demands, by Its very nature, that we affirmatively believe in and accept Its operation. It would be useless to argue why this is so, just as it would be useless to argue why there is a law of gravitation. These laws exist and all scientific advance is based on the supposition that any law of nature will respond to us when we comply with it.

When Jesus said that we should believe even before we receive, he was explaining the operation of the mental Law of cause and effect. If nothing is believed in It, then nothing is acted upon by It. But since there is such a Law, and since we are always believing something, the Law will always be operating upon what we believe, in the way we believe it. It is not that we introduce a new law, but that we bring the Law we are always using under conscious control, whether it be for ourselves or for someone else.

A practitioner is one who uses this Law for himself and for others. He uses It definitely, consciously and actively. His experience teaches him that implicit confidence and faith in the Law are the chief requirements for Its effective use. The experience of thousands has demonstrated this fact. And we can accept it. This is what we would do in dealing with other natural laws, and the Law of Mind in action is a natural law.

The Law is set in motion consciously. Its reaction is mechanical and mathematical. In such degree as one sees harmony instead of discord, he will demonstrate this harmony without having to create it. This is of utmost importance. Literally, man creates nothing at all, he merely uses creative forces. His obligation, having discovered the way laws work, is to use them intelligently. The responsibility for what is to take place is always in the law. Therefore, spiritual mind practice calls not only for definite attention and active awareness, but equally for a sort of relaxation because of implicit confidence in the Law.

Quite the reverse to the popular concept of holding thoughts, this calls for thinking them and then loosing them into the Law. The only will power used in the process—if it could be called will power—is a determination to keep the thought clear, to think about what ought to happen rather than about what ought not to happen, to be actively aware of harmony rather than discord, to believe that good will always overcome evil as light dissipates darkness.

There must be a calm confidence in our treatment. It is active but poised, conscious but balanced, definitely directed but not pushed into place. All declarations, all affirmations, all denials, all statements made in a treatment are for the sole purpose of clarifying the consciousness of the one who gives it.

The treatment for a person is definitely directed for that person, not *to* him but *for* him. Here is one of the main differences between psychology and metaphysics. There is but one mental Law of all life. The one who practices spiritual mind healing knows that he is directing It for a definite purpose but not pushing It out toward that purpose. What the Law of Mind knows in one place It knows simultaneously and instantly everywhere. It is equally distributed and everywhere present and Its manifestation appears at the point of our direction.

This practice is not mental coercion, it is not mental suggestion. It is mental awareness, a spiritual awareness of the mind. The mind is giving its consent. The mind is endeavoring to see the result already accomplished, to believe that it is already done.

Since the action of the Law is automatic and responds by

corresponding, or manifests through reflection, we need never wonder whether or not It operates. What we should pay attention to is our own inward awareness, building up an expectancy, increasing faith, stretching consciousness out, as it were, to include more.

Everything that is known about the Law of Mind substantiates the claim that a right state of consciousness can sublimate or transmute a negative state of consciousness. It is necessary that the spiritual mind practitioner assume authority in his work. His authority is the knowledge that the Law enforces Itself.

In actual practice, when a wrong condition does not seem to change it may be necessary to resort to a process of gradual conversion of thought from fear into faith. The scientific mind practitioner will not hesitate to do this when it is necessary. He looks upon the process, not as the thing itself, but as a way of arriving. The pathway is not the goal, but it helps him arrive at the goal.

If he can do away with the process and instantly arrive at the goal, well and good. If not, he must be willing to use a process until he does arrive. This is what constitutes scientific spiritual mind practice. Most of the results obtained in this field have been arrived at through this process and one should not condemn it because it does not measure up to his idea of absoluteness. He should be willing to use his technique and follow any process of thought necessary to arrive at the right conclusion.

When one assumes that a logical argument, based on the premise of spiritual perfection, presented to the field of Mind, will produce a definite result, he is making a true statement, the meaning of which will be understood when one realizes that the Law of Mind is merely a mechanical and mathematical reaction to one's thinking.

It cannot be said too often that a practitioner treats himself *for* someone else, always endeavoring to bring his own consciousness to a spiritual realization about the person he wishes to help. If this were not so, the practitioner would be handicapped by the thought that his patient might not receive his treatment or that he might refuse to accept it.

This calls for a calm and abiding trust in the Principle one uses and in his ability to use It. One does not have faith in himself, as an isolated human being. What he has faith in is the Principle. He has faith in himself only as he knows that he is using It correctly and that It will respond. He must have faith in his work or else he would be denying its effectiveness.

Spiritual mind practice is the very essence of faith. It is the essence of conviction—an act of assurance; a complete surrender of the will to a willingness to believe; a complete abandonment of thought to the Invisible. But the practitioner adds law to his faith and spiritual principles to his religion. He adds a conscious use of the Law of Mind to his conviction of the presence of Spirit.

In doing this he brings the personal to bear on the impersonal, which is Principle, while, at the same time, uniting his consciousness with the peace, the poise, the power, the beauty and the wisdom which the Spirit must be. Just as he knows that the law of the harvest will provide a crop, so he knows that the Law of Good will execute his word.

The Law is automatic and self-operative. The practitioner is not using Divine Mind to overcome a carnal mind. He is using a harmonious thought to overcome a discordant mental atmosphere. The basis of his work lies in the assumption that we are now living in a spiritual universe, that the law of our being is the Law of Mind in action, that there is an exact parallel between thoughts and things.

The practitioner must believe that the movement of mind acts as a movement of law. If he states in a treatment that his word is the law of elimination to a congested condition, he must believe that the congested condition is automatically eliminated through the law of his word. In the mind of the practitioner there should be no difference between stating, "This word is the law of elimination," and the elimination which should follow such a statement.

For instance, if a practitioner were treating one whose whole life is confused, he would not deal with the confusion but with the state of consciousness which causes it. He would clear away the thought of confusion and affirm peace. He would realize that law and order, harmony and peace, prevail in this man's life.

EXAMPLE

I know that I live in pure Spirit. I am one with the perfect Whole. Peace and calm surround me and flow through everything I do, say and think. There is a deep quiet at the center of my soul, a perfect poise and equilibrium. My thought rests upon everything in peace and joy and in cheerful expectation.

I know that (speaking the name of the patient) also lives in pure Spirit. At the center of his being is Peace, the Peace of the Spirit, and, underneath it all, the Love of the Divine Presence. As he becomes more conscious of this Love, all lack, all fear, all that is false, slips away as mists fade in the morning sunshine. He sees God in everything, personified in all people, manifest in every event. He is one with deep, abiding Peace. As this Peace flows through his being, every problem is released. He has an enthusiastic outlook on life and he permits himself to be guided into complete happiness. The way is made clear before him, and it is filled with joy and harmony.

One could not do this if he believed that things are independent of their silent, invisible causes. But if he really believes that the Law of Mind in action creates situations and conditions,

14

then he will know that, through changing the consciousness, he at the same time will be changing the condition. In other words, he must believe that causes and conditions are identical. The condition is a reflection of consciousness; the consciousness is the cause which reflects this condition.

If one watches this simple process in action he will discover that when treating someone who is surrounded by confusion, if he succeeds in clearing up all thought of confusion in his own mind, the circumstances surrounding the one he is working for will change. This change will be automatic and inevitable. This does not mean that there are secret or occult words which he uses. It means that any state of consciousness, consistently maintained, will produce a corresponding result.

Again we go back to the proposition that Divine Principle is a Law of Mind in action, which may be consciously used, while the Divine Presence is the infinite Spirit from whose all-light, wisdom and love one may draw inspiration, guidance and a sense of certainty. The practitioner performs a dual duty. One part of him is listening to this Divine Presence, the other is speaking his conviction into action through the Law. He must know with certainty that his word is the law of elimination to everything that contradicts the Divine Presence.

EXAMPLE

Realizing that the Infinite Spirit within me, which is God, the living Spirit Almighty, knows me as part of Itself, I consciously turn from every thought that can deny my union with all the presence, all the power, and all the good there is.

I know that my word, operating through the great Law of Life, is the law of my personal experience. I affirm my union with life, with love, with truth, with beauty and with power. I know everything I do, say and think is stimulated by Divine Intelligence, Infinite Love and Perfect

Wisdom. Nothing but good can go from me and only that which is good can return to me.

Calmly, joyfully, peacefully, I place myself in the hands of Divine Guidance, knowing I shall be stimulated to think intelligently, to choose wisely, and to act with precision. I rest in complete assurance that all is well with my soul, that all is well with the soul of everyone I contact, because God, the living Spirit, is over all, in all, and through all.

TECHNIQUE FOR PRACTICE

UNLESS THERE WERE A METHOD FOR SPIRITUAL MIND PRACTICE, then such practice would not be scientific. Unless there were a definite technique, its use could not be taught. Some people are fortunate enough to possess absolute conviction and faith through intuition. Such people are indeed fortunate. But all do not have this inward awareness. And if we waited for Divine Power to be released only through those few who possess this faith there would be little hope for the rest of us.

In metaphysical practice we arrive at this conviction through a process of thinking. The process itself is not the conviction, it is the road that leads to it. To the average individual this process is necessary. If he has an intelligent understanding of this science he will be willing to subject his mind to conscious self-training until there comes into his thinking a clearer realization of truth which the intuition feels and the intellect must, or may, proclaim.

In doing this one is not lessening the value of faith. Rather, he is recognizing it as the supreme affirmation of life. But knowing that he sees more or less as through a glass, darkly, he is willing to polish the glass, to wipe from its surface anything that blurs the passage of light through it. This is not a process of adjusting Reality to the condition that needs to be changed, but of adjusting the condition that needs to be changed to a Reality which already exists.

The physician or surgeon relies on nature to do the healing while he makes such mechanical adjustments as are necessary. The psychologist resolves mental and emotional conflicts that the mind may heal itself. The metaphysician also removes the obstructions and adjusts the condition to a greater reality.

The spiritual practitioner does not make a demonstration merely by saying peace where there is no peace. He makes a demonstration only when confusion is converted into peace. The authority of his words rests finally in what those words accomplish. It is the results that prove his theory.

For instance, suppose one is faced with the thought of discouragement or depression. Something within him knows that there is neither discouragement nor depression in the Divine Spirit. He makes some statements to this effect, but after having done so the confusion still persists. Now he resorts to a definite mental technique for using the Law of Mind in action. Where inspiration has failed he now begins to make certain statements.

EXAMPLE
God is neither depressed nor confused. There is no life apart from God. God is not afraid of anything.

At this point some image of fear may arise. He continues his treatment by saying:
There is no reality to this fear. There is nothing in my consciousness

that accepts it. There is no real law to enforce it, and none to believe in it.

He is presenting an argument to his mind, to his thought. He says:

My mind is the Mind of God. It is always calm and peaceful.

As he continues in such statements he finds he is lifting his mentality to a place where his vision becomes adjusted to a new viewpoint. He is demonstrating his position. He is adjusting experience to a fundamental harmony which exists in the universe.

There is no illusion about this for harmony begins to appear. Illusions can change but realities cannot. A knowledge of truth can dissipate an illusion. Illusion can never dissipate truth. The Divine Presence has never for one moment left any object, any person, any place or any thing, from the smallest to the greatest. The Divine Presence is always harmony and wholeness.

It is the reality of this Presence, the possibility of bringing It into one's conscious experience, that the practitioner must demonstrate. He is not fooling himself at all. Quite the reverse. He is becoming more intensely sane and the actual manifestation arising from his changed attitude is a complete proof of the rightness of his position. It is impossible for one to use this power without a deep and sincere spiritual conviction. He would have no principle to use unless he were conscious that thought, operating through conscious statements, enforces the Law of Mind and changes conditions.

Knowing this, the practitioner should not permit himself to be discouraged. An obstruction is but a challenge to his consciousness. Any condition that seems contrary to the Divine Harmony is but a challenge to his faith. Confusion is but a chal-

19

lenge to his feeling of confidence and trust.

If a practitioner worked on conditions as though they were causes in themselves or laws unto or within themselves, he would get nowhere. He would be subjecting his thought to the condition. Consequently, instead of changing the condition, he would be holding it in place. He knows that conditions are not things in themselves or laws unto themselves. He knows that all conditions are fluidic, they flow in and out, back and forth with thought. He converts the conditions into states of thought, and bringing a higher inward awareness to bear upon them, converts them to new conditions.

It will appear as though a miracle were taking place, as though Providence is granting him some special gift of life. But such is not the case. He is merely using a higher law, or, perhaps, the same law in a higher way. He is reversing his position in Mind. The Law of Mind is automatically reversing the conditions to meet the new state of awareness he has generated within his own consciousness.

Jesus was able to do this through pure, uplifted and holy faith. Many others have been able to do so in some lesser degree. Because comparatively few have been successful, the average person will have to resort to a conscious use of the Law of Mind in action. Here is a Principle that can be taught to anyone and used by anyone. There is no objection to calling it a principle of faith, provided we realize it is faith arrived at through understanding.

The Principle Jesus discovered and used we must use consciously. Because of superstition and ignorance, we have made his life the great exception instead of the great example. When his life becomes the great example rather than the great exception, all will use the same power he used. Some will use it better than others, but all can use it consciously. Anyone who uses it will get a result which mathematically equals, and mechanically corresponds to, his use of this Principle.

The basis for spiritual mind treatment is a conviction that man's life is pure Spirit. The practitioner recognizes this Spirit at the center of his patient's being. This Presence is more than a manifestation of God, it is God in that person. God is all in all. God is all power, all presence and all life. Life at the center of the patient's being is as perfect as it ever can become.

This Divine Presence has never been affected by anything external to Itself or different from Itself. Whatever process of reasoning one goes through to convince himself of this Divine Perfection is of no particular importance. It is a realization of this Perfection that heals.

The question might be asked, "Does one realize this Perfection by stating that it exists?" The answer is "Yes" and "No." If statements are real to the one who makes them, if he has a deep inward conviction and feeling, his statements have power. If the statements are merely intellectual equations, they have less power.

However, we should realize that in scientific practice we are using a definite technique. In making certain affirmations, and perhaps denials, the intellect is organizing itself for the purpose of coming to certain conclusions. It is as though the practitioner's argument were presented to a Mind Principle which acts upon the conclusions drawn in the practitioner's mind.

The mental practitioner removes the blocks and obstructions which hinder the manifestation of spiritual reality. The practitioner has a mental approach to a spiritual realization or recognition. He knows that thought responds to thought, that the whole field of consciousness is a combination of thought patterns operating as though they were laws unto themselves.

Since we as individuals are looking through our thought patterns, we are interpreting our world in light of these patterns. We are like one who, without knowing it, has put on some kind of glasses that invert everything so that in walking down the street the right side of the street might appear to be at the left, the sidewalk might appear to be up on top of the buildings, the sun might appear to rise in the west and set in the east.

Suppose we imagine someone wearing such glasses, and imagine that everything he looks at is inverted, is out of place. Even that which is true in itself assumes a false position. In reality this falseness is not the object of his perception but is his interpretation of that object. The Bible speaks of this as looking through a glass, darkly. Now he has become so accustomed to this inverted viewpoint that a true viewpoint would be shocking, it would be amazing, it would be unbelievable.

Suppose, then, we change the glasses and put on a pair that reveals things more nearly as they must be. He has to reverse his whole mental reaction. The sun is now rising in the east and setting in the west. The sidewalk is no longer on top of the buildings, and so with everything else in his experience.

It will be difficult for him to readjust his mental viewpoint to this new order, even though some deep rationality within him declares that he is now seeing straight for the first time. It almost seems as though he must put on the old glasses that he may again be in familiar surroundings. This is what Jesus referred to when he spoke of the blind leading the blind, with the inevitable result that both fall into the ditch.

It is said that some of the mystics and saints, when they were struck by the heavenly light, became so blinded that they could not see. They were compelled instantly to reverse their whole mental outlook on life. They found they had been looking at things, not into them. They had been looking upon themselves and others as separate from the Universal Self. One of the results of their experience was that, having received the heavenly light, their theology changed, their belief about the relationship between God and man was reversed. They had to adjust their intellectual vision of separation to a spiritual realization of unity.

A spiritual mind practitioner is one who intellectually and logically senses this unity and who has at least some spiritual awareness of its meaning. He has come to the conclusion that the glasses he and others have been wearing have inverted everything, they have misrepresented everything, they have borne false witness and the evidence has been so accepted that it has actually been experienced and is real enough from the standpoint of experience.

The spiritual mind practitioner must have enough inward vision or spiritual awareness to sense that there is a Divine Presence at the center of everything and that this Presence is perfect. It is the presence of this Reality that he seeks to demonstrate. He has taken off the old glasses, which invert everything, and put on new ones which cause everything to appear in its right place. Sometimes he seems to have on both pairs of glasses at the same time so that he looks at an object through the right lens and things are in place, and the next moment through the wrong lens and things seem out of place again.

Many people think that when one says that God is all there is he is denying the reality of things, of the physical body, the physical environment and even his own personality. This is not the case. The spiritual practitioner denies nothing other than wrong relationships. He does not deny the physical body or environment. He takes off the glasses that make things appear to be inverted and affirms a body of divine ideas ordained and organized by the supreme Spirit for the definite purpose of Its own self-expression. Therefore, he declares that everything in this body of ideas is in its proper place.

23

No matter how impossible any situation may seem or how difficult of solution any problem may appear, the practitioner holds to the idea that Spirit has no problems, there are no impossible situations. Sitting in quiet contemplation of Spirit, he fills himself with Its atmosphere.

EXAMPLE

I know that there is an inner Presence in everything. I know that this Presence responds to me. I know that everyone is an incarnation of God, that the living Spirit breathes through all. I recognize this Spirit and It responds to me. I realize that everything is alive, awake and aware with Spirit.

I commune with this Divine Presence. The Spirit within me reaches out and communes with the Spirit in everything and everyone I contact. It is the same Spirit in all, over all, and through all.

I have a deep realization that I am surrounded by an infinite Law which receives the impress of my thought and acts creatively upon it. I am conscious of my ability to use this Law, to direct it for specific purposes, for myself and others. There is nothing in me that can deny, limit, obstruct, divert or in any way hinder my use of this Law. It is within my own mind, because God is right where I am.

In calm confidence, in perfect trust, in abiding faith and with complete peace, I let go of every problem, as a problem. I receive the answer as fulfillment.

As a general principle the practitioner feels that any wrong condition is a direct opposite of what should be. In doing this he may deny the wrong position. He adjusts his thinking, his mental seeing and inward feeling, to the proposition that everything, rightly understood, is part of a whole harmony, of a complete unity. He may deny everything that seems wrong and affirm its direct Opposite.

24

The practitioner must be careful, in meeting the negative, that he does not make it positive by too emphatic a denial of it. What he denies is a shadow, not a substance; a false conclusion, not the truth. His denial is merely brushing aside the evidence of confusion, of uncertainty and doubt, until he sees that they are neither person, place nor thing, neither law, cause, medium nor effect. To him, they must be as nothing claiming to be something, a lie claiming to be the truth.

It is in this sense that there is something uncompromising about spiritual mind practice. Consider the words of Jesus when he said, "Heaven and earth shall pass away, but my words shall not pass away." Think of this man who dared to stand alone in the waste places of human consciousness, who dared to look through the physical and mental to the spiritual cause, who dared to tell Lazarus to come out of his tomb!

In treatment we should withdraw all personal opinions from our thinking. Let us use the illustration of setting a physical object on a table. While we may move the object from one place to another, we are not forcing or coercing the law of gravitation; we are merely changing our position in it. It is in this sense that we should get ourselves out of the way when giving a treatment.

We do not destroy the laws of life. They are always there, appearing to us when we use them. If we realize that peace is at the center of our being, no matter how much confusion we may have been experiencing, then the peace which never departed will become apparent. This peace does not really reassert itself, because it never ceased asserting itself, it was always there. We were merely looking at it in a confused manner.

If we look at a confused situation until confusion disappears from our consciousness, peace alone will remain. Any statement about peace, any realization of its presence, will help us. The power is not so much in the statements we use as in the consciousness they induce. They help us to become aware of that which already is. As one statement of truth after another is made, the images of discord and confusion are dissipated and peace becomes apparent.

Every treatment a practitioner gives tends to strengthen his own consciousness, to uplift his soul to the Divine embrace. A practitioner is a spiritual mind adventurer in the almost unexplored country of absolute cause. If he felt the result of his work depended on anything personal, he would surely fail. It is only as he throws himself, in complete abandonment, into a consciousness of realization that his words become effective.

One practicing this science is always endeavoring to conform his thinking to a spiritual ideal. He must train himself to be aware of the Divine Spirit at the center of his patient's life. His arguments, statements, affirmations or denials are arranged to disclose the reality of this spiritual Presence, to make It real, to feel It. There is a spiritual logic higher than the intellect. Every man has an intuition about this and unconsciously senses its reality. In practice one consciously guides the intellect to this spiritual perception.

The practitioner clears up his own thought *for* someone else. The reaction in the other person will be equal to the realization in the mind of the practitioner. Since the medium of Mind is universal and a complete unit, it makes no difference where the other person may be. The practitioner states that his word is *for* this particular person. He should not think of it as being *to*, but *for*, him. Should he think of it as being *to* that person he will almost unconsciously try to send out thoughts or to influence the other person's mind. This is not scientific mental practice. *Scientific mental practice begins and ends in the consciousness of the one giving a treatment.* It is for someone else when he is treating another person. It is for himself when he is treating himself.

26

In such degree as one becomes aware of the spiritual perfection of his patient, this awareness is transmitted to the patient and operates through him, eliminating his wrong beliefs and their negative results. In such degree as one is able to clear up his own thought about another, he will discover a corresponding clarity of thought in the mind of the one for whom he is working.

EXAMPLE

Saying to yourself the name of the one you wish to help, speak to your own consciousness about him:

This person is now spiritually perfect. Every organ, every action and every function of his physical being is part of the Divine Order. There is perfect circulation, perfect assimilation and perfect elimination. There is one life, that life is God, that life is his life now. It is flowing through him, happily, harmoniously, completely.

Now make any other statements which help you to realize that the person you are working for is a spiritual being and is now manifesting the harmony, the peace and the wholeness which you believe the Spirit must be.

If a patient is suffering from fear, it is not an effective treatment merely to say that God has no fear. The practitioner must know that there is no fear in the person he wishes to help. His knowledge that God-Life, at the center of his patient, is free from fear, is the Principle he wishes to demonstrate, the basis on which his treatment is given. He now definitely and deliberately removes fear from his consciousness about the patient.

Knowing that thoughts are things, and that states of consciousness produce their logical results, a practitioner formulates his statements in such a manner that his own consciousness becomes aware of the Divine Presence, the activity of the Law, and the definite accomplishment of its purpose. He is following the instruction laid down by the Great Teacher who said that when you pray you must believe that you already possess that for which you pray.

This would be no different from saying that if you wish a harvest you must first plant, you must put the idea in the creative soil. Shifting this over into the field of Mind, we arrive at the conclusion that the idea must be accepted as an already accomplished fact because the Law knows no season of time, It can only operate on the concept held in It. He is the best practitioner who best understands this and who best has trained himself to have complete confidence, both in the Spirit and in the Law.

In the activity of his consciousness the practitioner arrives at a place in his thought where he passes the whole proposition over to the Law and joyfully leaves it there. This is quite different from the popular concept of holding thoughts or of concentrating some power. There is nothing to concentrate and nothing to hold. There is merely something to become aware of.

EXAMPLE

I now let Divine Power flow through me. I permit the Divine Spirit to fill me with Its perfect life. I have complete faith in God, therefore I relax into the realization that I am bathed in pure Spirit, in living Life, in everlasting Goodness. I accept the circulation of Divine Life, Love and Energy flowing through my whole being. As this Divine Life flows through me it eliminates everything that does not belong to Its own perfect being.

He then applies this state of consciousness to the person for whom he is working:

This person lives in a consciousness of good. He has a complete sense of security, of happiness, of love, of wholeness and divine protection. He has complete faith in God. He is now surrendering everything that does not belong to his physical body to the Divine Life, knowing that anything that does not belong will be eliminated.

He has a deep sense of joy, of enthusiasm, of the love of life. He feels the pulsation, the rhythm of this life in every atom of his being. He feels the joy and the energy of it in every action. A deep sense of love, peace and joy fills his entire being with radiant life, with light and with power. He permits the Divine Life to flow through him and he is made whole because God in him is perfect.

It is useless to make statements in a spiritual mind treatment that we do not inwardly believe. All statements must flow out of a consciousness of conviction. The words used are merely a spontaneous expression of our inward beliefs about life. They must flow from the entire consciousness, the whole mental life, the entire mental process. Spiritual consciousness means that when the intellect affirms the Divine Presence the whole consciousness feels the meaning of what the intellect has affirmed.

This training of consciousness is not only important in this practice, it is the chief characteristic of it. Our consciousness is not at all times inwardly aware of goodness, truth and beauty, and here is where scientific or conscious mental practice performs its important office. The practitioner knows that conscious right thought, brought to a focus through definite statements, enforces the Law of Mind. He has knowledge of a science which can be used by any intelligent person provided he complies with its principle and law. He has a definite technique that can be used and he has a conscious knowledge of how to proceed.

Life is and we live it. The Law of Mind is and we use it. The teacher or practitioner of this science, like those in physical sciences, need not explain *why* things are so. No physicist attempts to explain why energy is. He merely accepts the fact that it is and uses it. Just as many years of careful work and experiment in the field of science have established certain truths and developed certain techniques, so in spiritual mind practice many years of investigation have demonstrated the principle and practice in this field.

We know something of the *how*, nothing of the *why*. The *how* we use, the *why* we must accept. In doing this we are in no way departing from scientific procedure because all science must follow the same method. Prayer and faith have produced wonders throughout the ages. We are reducing them to a principle which can be, at least in some degree, consciously understood. Faith *is* a principle in the universe, and wherever it has been exercised, this principle has been demonstrated.

WORDS USED IN TREATMENT

ALL STATEMENTS USED IN TREATMENT MUST BE FELT WITH A feeling beyond words, beyond statements and phrases. It is from the essence of this feeling of Life and Spirit that the mind draws its conclusions, which, presented to the Mind Principle, causes It to react in an affirmative rather than a negative way. Feeling results in words, thoughts and ideas which are the activity of this feeling, which words, thoughts and ideas become the enforcement of the Law of Mind in action. In this way the word becomes a law of Spirit and Life.

Right spiritual knowing is an intelligent activity of thought which reveals pure Spirit as the invisible cause of everything. Right knowing gives rise to right thinking. Right thinking projects an inward state of pure feeling. An atmosphere of reality is loosed through the word which projects as much reality as one feels at that moment. It produces a result equal to his inward awareness.

31

Why must a treatment be consciously directed? The answer is self-evident. If you have faith, you must have faith in something. Consciousness must be conscious of something. Therefore, no matter how high one's consciousness may be, it will still remain merely an atmosphere in consciousness unless it is directed. "He sent out his word and healed him."

In treatment words are always specific and direct because consciousness must be conscious of something. The practitioner feels something which cannot be stated in words, and, at the same time, directs his spiritual awareness for specific purposes. Specific intention is necessary in effective treatment. The words, thoughts or ideas focus this intention for a definite purpose.

Since words without meaning have no power, we must realize that the word of power is a word that has embodied power. The word is merely a spontaneous exclamation of that power. One need not be concerned over the particular words he uses but he should be concerned over their meaning.

The practitioner applies this meaning to the person he is working for or the condition he is working with. When he says that the action of Spirit (right action) is operating through the affairs of the one he is working for, he must inwardly sense that right action is taking place in the affairs of that person. He must know that the word he speaks is the Law of Mind operating for this person.

This entire action takes place in the mind of the one giving the treatment. He is inwardly aware of his own union with good, trying to sense what this union means, feeling it in his thought, realizing it deep in his being. It is from this deep realization that he gives his treatment, knowing that each word must find an outlet which corresponds to the inner meaning of that word.

He is not attempting to coerce the Spirit or compel the

Law. The Spirit is always willing and the Law is always ready. It automatically flows around everything. It needs merely to be recognized and used. This is the general atmosphere of a treatment.

EXAMPLE

Realizing that my word is the presence, the power and the activity of the living Spirit in and through me, I speak this word with complete confidence that it is the law of good unto (the person, place or condition) *for which it is spoken.*

I know there is but one Life, that Life is God, that Life is the life of the person of whom I am now thinking. Every organ, action and function of his physical being is rooted in a divine reality, has a pattern in the spiritual world which is now perfect, and I know there is nothing within him, or within me, that can deny or obstruct this divine reality which flows with complete freedom through his entire being.

As this spiritual circulation takes place, everything which does not belong to the divine and perfect Life is eliminated, calmly, joyfully, peacefully. I realize this divine action and know that it is good.

These are merely words suggesting certain thoughts and feelings which must be real in the mind of the practitioner. He does not think of the particular words he is going to use in the treatment, but he does have a certain feeling that automatically expresses itself in words. It is a combination of feeling and words that produces the desired result.

He will never use the same words twice, nor need he ever be too consciously aware of the words he uses at any time. Just as one seeking to describe a certain situation does not think out in advance exactly what he is going to say, but merely begins to express his thought and feeling about such a situation, so, in a very definite sense, the practitioner talks to himself about a person or situation, and out of his own spiritual awareness convinces his own mind.

The practitioner should feel that all the power in the universe is back of his words and flowing through them. One could not feel this way if he thought he were dealing with will power, mental coercion, concentration or mental suggestion; with the influence of mind on mind or the influence of mind over matter.

There should be a sense of joy in this work, a feeling of enthusiasm as well as conviction, a warm mental expectancy backed by a deep intellectual conviction, and an even deeper spiritual awareness. This inner state of awareness is something each one must work out for himself, within himself. There are many guides, such as reading the words of Jesus and other spiritual geniuses, and trying to enter into the meaning of their thoughts. It is this meaning of the words used that is important in practicing the Science of Mind.

An artist may be taught techniques. He may learn mechanical methods. He can be shown how to set up a canvas, how to draw an outline. He can be taught perspective and how to mix colors. But even the greatest master cannot teach an artist how to feel. Feeling must flow up from within or there will be no beauty on his canvas. There is something that he cannot be taught, something that must come from his own inward feeling as he reaches out toward the essence of beauty.

There is an artistry in spiritual mind healing, a feeling, a sentiment, a spiritual emotion. No one can give this to us but ourselves. No merely superficial viewpoints, no mere philosophy of life, no mere logic or reason can do this for one. There is an inward witness in everyone that alone can do this. The Spirit Itself must bear witness to the fact.

The mind must swing between meditation, conscious communion with the Spirit, and action. It must swing between real-ization and statement, between feeling and words, between meaning, which is interior awareness, and thoughts, which are the tools of this awareness.

The words, the thoughts, the statements used in a treatment give form to feeling, while the conscious intention for which these statements are made gives direction to the treatment. In this way, feeling is caught in form, while words, through definite intention, specialize this feeling for concrete purposes. This is what is meant by letting the Spirit bear witness to the words while the words give direction to the Law.

EXAMPLE

I know this person whom I am treating is a divine, spiritual being. He lives and moves in pure Spirit. He is one with love, with peace, with joy and with life. Everything that he does, says or thinks is governed by pure Intelligence and inspired by Divine Wisdom. He is guided into right action. He is surrounded with friendship, love and beauty. Enthusiastic joy, vitality and inspiration are in everything he does.

He represents that Life which cannot want, which is forever mani-festing freedom, self-expression and wholeness. He represents the princi-ple of Divine Activity which never tires, which is birthless, changeless and deathless. He is receptive to the inexhaustible energy of the universe, to the influx of perfect life, perfect ideas, and complete joy.

He is conscious of divine guidance, of complete happiness, abundant health and increasing prosperity. He is aware of his partnership with the Infinite. He knows that everything he does shall prosper.

He accepts this word. He knows that it is the presence, the power and the activity of God in him. He knows he is conscious of divine guidance, of inward peace and poise. He immediately becomes conscious of a more abundant life. He expects greater good, more happiness, and a complete success in every constructive thing which he undertakes.

Again I affirm that this word, being the presence of the Spirit in him, is the Law of God operating through him, and establishes in him that which is good, beautiful and true.

It is done. I accept. I believe. I know.

FUNCTION OF FAITH

NOTHING HAPPENS BY CHANCE IN THE UNIVERSE. EVERYTHING is in accord with law. Faith is a law, and acts as such. The law of faith is a law of belief—a belief so complete that the mind no longer rejects it. This belief must be subjective as well as objective. It must penetrate our inner consciousness.

The practitioner has a complete conviction that a higher use of the Law of cause and effect transcends a lower use of it. Even though he starts with only an intellectual or logical conviction of this, a spiritual intuition within him will support this logic and give him a consciousness of its reality. This will lift his faith to a place of complete certainty. Spiritual consciousness should be added to mental technique. Mental technique is the use we make of this consciousness.

The practitioner must know that conditions flow from causes and not the reverse, that everything in the physical world is an effect which must have a mental and spiritual cause back of it.

He changes the cause and the Law changes the fact. It is only where there is a realization of the supremacy of spiritual thought force over what seems to resist it that there is any power in a treatment.

It might be asked if this is different from faith. Only in the sense that it is faith used as understanding, faith consciously applied for definite purposes, faith definitely directed to specific ends. When Jesus multiplied the loaves and fishes he was not turning water into wine; he was not finding money in the fish's mouth or healing the blind man. He was multiplying loaves and fishes. He was using his spiritual awareness for the definite purpose of feeding the multitude. He multiplied the idea in his own consciousness, gave thanks, and with sublime indifference told them to distribute the result among the multitude.

This was, indeed, an act of unconditioned faith, but it was a definite faith. He was doing a specific thing. Jesus was definite in his use of spiritual power. When he told the blind man to see he was using his consciousness of spiritual vision for the purpose of changing blindness into sight. The blindness was an objective condition which he ignored. His mental and spiritual equivalent of seeing was greater than the man's mental equivalent of not being able to see, therefore, it transcended it and immediately the man's eyes were opened.

One who studies the acts of faith through the ages discovers that effective faith has always been applied to specific purposes when definite results have followed. There is an authentic story of a man who prayed for God to lift a fog. He was entering a harbor and the captain of his boat refused to dock in the fog. This man of great spiritual faith took the captain into his cabin and prayed with him that the fog might be lifted. When they went on deck it had cleared away. This man was a good, old-fashioned, orthodox preacher, but he was complying with the law of faith. He was seeing through the fog to the light.

A practitioner of spiritual mind healing is continually confronted with the fog of fear, superstition and doubt; otherwise, there would be no occasion for his practice. He will either get lost in the fog, or see through it. Though the fog is there, the sun is always shining—this is what he clings to. He declares that the sun is shining and that the fog is dissipated. This is his act of faith, his compliance with the Law, his surrender of appearances to a greater certainty in his own consciousness.

Because this is so, the spiritual mind practitioner must spend much time alone in quiet meditation until Spirit becomes as real to him as form. Spiritual mind practice does not call for great concentration, but for deep realization and conviction.

If this deep conviction were something we had to implant in our minds we should be lost in a sea of speculative philosophy. The wonderful thing about this is that the deep conviction is already there when we clear away the confusion. If one had to put life into Life he couldn't do it, he would be lost. But if Life is already at the center of everything, one can recognize It. This is what spiritual mind practice is. It is the recognition of a deep and abiding harmony at the center of everything.

EXAMPLE

I have a deep and abiding conviction that there is one divine and perfect Presence in the universe; that the spirit of Truth is everywhere; that God is right where I am. There is neither doubt, confusion, nor fear, for I know I am rooted in the one and only perfect and divine Presence.

I also realize that the divine Law of Life operates upon my word to bring about definite results in my affairs and the affairs of those for whom I am thinking. I have a complete confidence in this Law of Good, an unshakable trust in It, and complete reliance upon It. I know, as Jesus said, that "all things are possible to God;" that there is no limitation to the Law of Good. Therefore, in quiet confidence, in calmness and peace, and in perfect trust, I speak my word (that is, I say these words, make these affirmations, or give this treatment for myself or for some person, situation or condition).

If the treatment is for oneself, he says:

I am conscious that I am surrounded by Divine Love and Infinite Wisdom, and that the Life of God is my life now. I know that there is nothing in me which can hinder Divine Intelligence from governing my affairs, from daily guiding me into right action, therefore, I affirm that at all times I know what to do and am impelled intelligently to act on every right impression that comes to me.

In this there is no labor, no strain, no anxiety, but rather, complete realization and calmness because the practitioner has absolute confidence in the Law and should have equal confidence in his ability to use It. He should know that his word is the operation of the Law as he designates it. Having translated the material universe into terms of thought or consciousness, realizing that all manifest effects are merely consciousness in form, he generates a consciousness of right action, knowing that the Law of Life will automatically create conditions which will be exact physical correspondents to his inward mental attitude.

It is necessary for the practitioner to withdraw his thought from things as they appear to be and to think independently of any and all existing conditions. No one can hope successfully to practice this science unless he is able and willing to do this.

Is this not an act of faith? Most certainly it is. And so is everything else in life. We have faith that the laws of nature will work. We have faith that when we plant a seed it will produce a plant. We have faith that the law of gravitation will hold everything in place. The only thing that we are adding to this faith is a realization that all natural laws are rooted in Divine Intelligence, that natural laws are Divine Intelligence operating. Our own word, affirmation, prayer or faith is another one of these natural laws operating in the field of consciousness.

The practitioner withdraws from the contemplation of existing circumstances, and without contending against them, actually creates a new set of circumstances through consciously reversing the law that produced the conditions which ought to be changed. If his mind dwelt only on things as they appear to be, he would never demonstrate beyond that appearance and everything that happened would merely be more of the same thing.

But he steps his consciousness up, sees through and beyond the fact to the new cause. He sometimes denies the fact merely to brush it out of his thought while he affirms its opposite.

Faith is a mental attitude toward life which can be cultivated. It can be consciously acquired. Any desired state of consciousness can be acquired if we work at it long enough. If this could not be done there would be no Science of Mind or Spirit. Once we realize that faith is subject to definite laws, and that these laws are laws of mind in action, we shall see that faith can be consciously generated.

We cannot be too definite about this. It is the very substance of conscious spiritual mind practice and it can be definitely taught. All people who have exercised effective faith throughout the ages have used this law, whether they were conscious of it or not. We are merely trying to bring the law of faith under conscious control. Rightly viewed, this is not so much an attempt to acquire faith as it is to use a faith which everyone already possesses.

We should seek to combine spiritual up-reaching with conscious mental action for definite purposes. This is what constitutes spiritual mind practice on a scientific basis. And by "scientific" we do not mean anything cold or merely mechanical. We merely mean the conscious use of a known law.

We are, in our outside world, a result of the subjective state of our thought. The acquired subjective, and perhaps largely unconscious, thought patterns which we entertain are continually impinging upon our environment, attracting and repelling without our conscious awareness. The subconscious content of one's thought determines what is going to happen to him. It seems to be the medium between the Absolute and the relative in our experience. In such degree as we re-educate our habitual thought patterns they will automatically react in accord with a mechanical mental law, a law of reflection.

The average person is ignorant of these facts about our spiritual life, and, unfortunately, many who do believe in them are superstitious about spiritual mind practice. Many think we are persuading God or manipulating the Spirit when we give a mental treatment. All such ideas should be discouraged and we should come to see that spiritual mind treatment is the conscious use of a definite law.

Right practice includes correct teaching because we not only wish to help people, we should have an equal desire to teach them how to help themselves. People should be shown how to unite faith with understanding so that they will not only know *what* they are doing, but *how* and *why* they are doing it. Their faith is in God, the living Spirit. It is both right and necessary that they have this faith. Their knowledge, however, is of a definite Law of cause and effect in the mental world, the Law of Mind in action.

Jesus made repeated references to the action of this Law. He said: Thy faith hath made thee whole ... Do you believe this can be done? If you do, it can ... Heaven and earth shall pass away, but my words shall not pass until all be fulfilled. In the parable of the sower he referred to the word as the seed. Undoubtedly he understood the action of this Law, but knowing that It responds by corresponding, he told his followers to stay close to the Spirit, then there could be nothing in the automatic reaction of the Law to produce harm.

Jesus laid down the whole law as one of belief. He made it so simple that its meaning has eluded us. We have wondered by what special act of grace or Divine Providence he was able to heal the sick, turn water into wine, or multiply loaves and fishes. Jesus did not reverse the laws of nature. He reversed the common use of them. He was not merely a man who *had* great faith. He *used* his faith in a positive rather than a negative way. His faith in good was equal to the average man's faith in evil. It was not a different faith; it was a different *use* of faith.

When one is working for spiritual results he should keep his counsel to himself, not arguing with others lest he enter into their unbelief. His spiritual awareness is a secret in his own mind. It must not receive suggestions of negation from any source. He clings to the mental images of good, disregarding any apparent opposite, whether it be in mind or in form, in thought or in affairs.

With a childlike confidence, the practitioner lifts up his consciousness to the universe. This sublime act of faith is justified by its results, for the universe honors our acceptance of it in the terms of that acceptance.

EXAMPLE

I know that the Spirit within me is God. I let this Spirit, which is perfect, complete and whole, flow through me. I let the spirit of love and peace permeate my entire being, desiring only that which is good, seeing only that which is good.

I have faith that my word shall not return unto me void. I surrender myself completely to this faith, for I know that there is a creative Spirit which gives substance to this faith and which will provide the evidence of this substance in actual fact. I know that my faith operates through an immutable Law and that there is no possibility whatsoever of its failing. I expect, then, to meet my good, and I rejoice in the anticipation of this good.

I know that good alone can go from me and return to me, therefore, I rest in calmness and confidence, knowing that Divine Love and Infinite Intelligence will guide and guard.

SPIRITUAL AWARENESS

IN A CERTAIN SENSE SPIRITUAL MIND HEALING IS A REVELATION in that it is designed to reveal the real nature of the person for whom one is working. No matter what the process through which one goes in working for a patient, he is always working for a realization, in his own mind, of the spiritual nature of the one he wishes to help. It makes little difference what method one pursues in arriving at spiritual realization. The method is the way, the road he travels. The destination is the awareness.

All the words, thoughts, affirmations and denials; the declarations and realizations, in a spiritual mind treatment are for the purpose of bringing the consciousness of the practitioner to a higher level of spiritual acceptance. Words are molds. It is the consciousness which flows through them that fills these molds with a living substance.

The important factor, then, is whether or not the form that one uses causes his own mind to believe. He may use a process of reasoning, of logic, or argument with himself. He may go through a process of affirmation and denial. But always the process should tend toward the gaining of an inward realization, a feeling, a sense, an atmosphere of peace, harmony and protection.

His entire treatment is based on the assumption that there is a spiritual pattern at the center of everything. The perfect was always there, it was implanted by the Spirit. The imperfect has been added by the human mind. What the human mind has put there, it can take away. What the Divine has implanted cannot be uprooted; it can only appear to be covered up. Spiritual mind practice is an uncovering of the Divine Nature.

If his work is to be effective, the practitioner must believe this. Unless, through a simple, direct act of faith he instantly feels the Divine center, then he must resort to a method. To practice with assurance of consistent results one cannot depend entirely on the inspiration of the moment. He must have a method of procedure, a way to arrive at spiritual awareness through a process of statements.

EXAMPLE

I am conscious that the life and the intelligence within me is some part of the Universal Spirit. Therefore, I know that my mind is one with the Infinite Mind. Being one with the Infinite Mind, it is continuously guided and directed and all my actions are controlled by the Spirit within me.

I know exactly what to do in every situation. Every idea necessary to successful living is brought to my attention. The doorway to ever-increasing opportunity for self-expression is ever open before me. I am continuously meeting new and larger experiences. Every day brings some greater good. Every day brings more blessing and greater self-expression. I am prospered in everything I do. An abundance of good is mine today.

There is that within me which understands the Truth, which completely accepts It, which remembers freedom, expresses freedom, and anticipates freedom. There is that within me which is completely conscious of its unity with good, of its oneness with all the power there is, all the presence there is, and all the life there is. Upon this Power, Presence and Life I depend with complete certainty. I have absolute inner assurance that Divine Intelligence guides me in everything I do.

I know there is an inner Presence in everyone and in everything. I know that this Presence responds to me. I know that everyone is an incarnation of God, that the living Spirit breathes through all. I realize that everything is alive, awake and aware with Spirit. I recognize this Spirit and It responds to me. The Spirit within me reaches out and communes with the Spirit in everyone and everything I contact. It is the same Spirit in all, over all, and through all.

Spiritual awareness is important in the use of the Law of Life for the Law is a servant of the Spirit. Our spiritual awareness is the secret place of the most High within us. Our conviction and faith are the Mount of Transfiguration where we receive a deep conviction that there is a Spirit in man and that this Spirit is God.

Since so much in the world contradicts this, the one seeking to demonstrate the principle of good must spend much time in the silence of his own thought, gathering into himself the spiritual energies of the universe until they become more real to him than that which contradicts them. There seems to be no shortcut. Since everyone is an individual, each must generate his own consciousness and establish his own spiritual equilibrium.

Jesus said that the door to the larger life is always open. He must have meant that heaven is ever-present with us. Always, at the other side of confusion there is peace; always, at the other side of disturbance there is poise; always, evil is dissipated by good, if we persistently view good instead of evil. This may appear madness to the intellect which has accustomed itself to accepting things as they appear to be. To the intellectually blind, spiritual awareness seems folly, just as faith is folly to fear or happiness folly to disillusionment or health to disease.

The universe can only give us what we take, and since our taking is a thing of consciousness, the universe can only give us what we are aware of. No doubt our eternal evolution is an everlasting process through which we become more aware of life. It is at least a thing of joy to contemplate that no matter how much good we may be experiencing today, it is but a forerunner of more good.

But if we are fulfilling ourselves today and filling the present with happiness and the highest sense of wholeness we can entertain, we are doing well. The logical sequence of the much and more will take place in due time. We are not yet ready for more than we can understand, and when we understand and embody the more, it will be there.

It is as though we were dipping up water from a limitless sea. Each day we may use a larger measure and each day dip up more. The ocean will never become exhausted. As a matter of fact, everything we dip up will again run back into it, only to take a new form. Thus the play of Life goes on within Itself forever—spontaneous self-realization flowing from an infinite sea of self-knowingness.

We should think of our lives as an increasing awareness, an ever-growing and expanding consciousness, a never ceasing progress of individual and collective evolution. There should be a constant joy in expansion, an enthusiastic sense of adventure in the progressive unfoldment of spiritual awareness. It is enough to know that our good is with us today, that tomorrow this same good can be multiplied, and so on forever.

This is a true spiritual relationship with the universe, for God is not some far-off event, but an ever-present reality. We should not think of the Spirit as separate from us, but as within as well as around us. While we entertain the concept of a God who is distant our search will be to reunite ourselves with the Divine Source of our being. It is not really union with God that we are searching after. The search *after* union is merely one of the intellectual steps we take. Gradually this search after union must cease and we must learn to live from a unity which is forever established.

This has been the secret of the lives of the mystics throughout the ages. Those who have been blessed with cosmic consciousness no longer say, "I will go in search of Him," but rather, "This is what He is." As Jesus said, "Who hath seen me hath seen the Father." Not all of the Father, of course, but that which is of like nature to the parent mind. These too few people, whose words and thoughts we study as pearls of great price, have so blended their thought and feeling with the Invisible that the very essence of Its being has proclaimed Its nature through them.

Let us see how this works. Let us consider the life of one who has been more or less consumed with jealousy, hatred, bickering and resentment. He has become so isolated that love neither flows from nor to him. Human affection itself appears to have dried up at the source.

If he is an intelligent person he will realize this. He will know that something is wrong. Because life has implanted intuition within him, he senses that there is something which could readjust him to Life in such a way that he would be loved, be happy. If he is rightly guided, either through his own intuition or by someone else, he will begin to travel backward within himself to see where the trouble lies (for trouble always lies, it never tells the truth). Through faith or understanding he determines to retrace his mental steps, to go back in imagination to the place where he is one with all.

EXAMPLE

"I will fear no evil for thou art with me." Today Divine Love and infinite tenderness sustain me. In order that I shall not separate myself from this love, I endeavor to see it reflected in everyone and everything. I shall permit only that which is loving, kind and true to find entrance or exit through my consciousness. Thus I shall be assured that I am bathed in the warm glow of that Love which casts out all fear.

Today I bestow the essence of love upon everything. Everyone shall be lovely to me. My soul meets the soul of the universe in everyone. Nothing is ugly; everything is beautiful, everything is meaningful. This love is a healing power touching everything into wholeness, healing the wounds of experience with its divine balm.

I know that this Love Essence, the very substance of Life, the creative Principle back of everything, flows through my whole being, spiritual, emotional, mental and physical. It flows in transcendent loveliness into my world of thought and form, ever renewing, vitalizing, bringing joy and harmony and blessing to everything and everyone it touches.

Although it is not easy, something stimulates him to persist in this effort, so he gradually reverses his thoughts about people. He comes into harmony with life. He unifies with living. He begins to see good in everything. As he does this, the good that was already in him, the love that had merely been wearing the mask of hate, the jealousies, animosities and resentments which had been born of a sense of isolation, disappear. The love which was already there comes to the surface.

People begin to see that a great change has come over him, that, after all, he is not such a bad person, there is much in him

to admire. Gradually, this thought changes from one of specula-
tion to one of confidence, from one of intellectual analysis to
one of deep emotional response, and finally, to one of spiritual
awareness whereby people see in him the embodiment of love,
of kindness, of sympathy and of fellowship.

He has found union with love. He no longer seeks it. He is
it, therefore, its being passes through him. Can we say that the
love we now experience in him is any different from, or other
than, that love we ascribe to the Divine Being Itself?

We should not feel that this divine beneficence is ordained
for a few. It is the gift of heaven to all. This is the very essence
of religion. No religion can have this essence unless it is found-
ed in love. It is wonderful to contemplate that one may realize
such love, unify with it, and live from it.

There can be no effective, no lasting results of spiritual mind
treatment unless it reunites the soul with its Source. We cannot
divorce spiritual realization from the most effective form of
mental treatment. Unless the mind becomes converted to a realization of the Spirit it is still struggling in isolation. The mental
practitioner can have hope of success only as he believes in, and
lives from, the indwelling Spirit.

The thought that reaches the highest level will have the
greatest power. The very fact that the Law of Mind is like any
other mechanical law in nature, and operates mathematically,
shows us that the Law, of Itself, can do nothing for us other than
automatically leveling Its reaction at the highest point of our
inward awareness. *Spiritual consciousness is power.*

The demonstration made through the Law is merely the logical outcome of a consciousness acquired through the Spirit. We
cannot divorce spiritual realization from the highest use of this
Law, and there would be no use in trying. It would be like trying to take the heat out of fire or rob the sun of its light. When

we realize that the Law of Mind in action is a mechanical force, all sense of compulsion or trying to make things happen will disappear from our consciousness. We shall proceed on the assumption that thoughts and things are identical. Our time will be spent more in acquiring a consciousness than Ill trying to make things happen.

This will in no way exclude the acquirement of things, for everything that gives us happiness is right, everything that gives joy is in accord with nature, everything that produces loveliness, peace and contentment must belong to the Divine Kingdom. These things are included in a consciousness of the Kingdom and we should have no hesitation in announcing the accomplishment, through law, of any legitimate desire. But always back of these things which make for the fuller life there must be a growing consciousness of the whole, a deepening conviction of the power of good, a growing realization of the Divine Presence.

If we were making the statement: "God is all there is," it would be more complete in our consciousness if we were to add: "God is right here now." When we say, "The activity of Spirit is the only activity there is," we complete the statement by saying: "This activity is right here in this condition."

In treatment we bring our highest concept of Life to a focal point, declaring that since Life is unconditioned, whole and forever flowing, It is flowing in right action through the person, place or thing we are thinking about. In this way we bring heaven to earth.

There is a deeper level than the intellect, yet, it is the intellect that must unite with that something larger than itself. The intellect is not to become lost, but found, in a universal wholeness. The self discovers the self in a larger self. It is the earnest desire of every worker in this field to make this self-discovery for himself and others. One who listens to the gentle urgings of his

52

own soul and accustoms himself to seeing God in all nature will gradually be transforming himself from a lower to a higher consciousness of life.

The practitioner must not only know that he is one with Life, there should be a sense of Life flowing through him. The words he uses should impart an atmosphere of something greater than these words, something which has a deeper meaning than anything he could put into words. The words are merely a proclamation of this meaning, shaped at any particular time to meet a particular need.

Our approach to the Spirit should be simple, direct and spontaneous. There is no more of God in one place than in another. Wherever we are, there God is, and wherever we recognize the Divine Presence, then the Divine Presence responds.

To trust in this Presence is the highest form of sanity. To feel that It is guiding us is normal. To desire that the Divine Mind shall project Itself in our thought and act is natural. It is that spiritual something which must be added to every word spoken in effective mental treatment. Everyone should train himself to listen deeply to the Spirit which spontaneously flows through his own being. This is adding the Spirit of Truth to the letter of the Law. When the two become one, the most amazing power the world has ever witnessed flows freely into action through human affairs.

This is the goal toward which the mind of every practitioner travels, whether he is working for himself or someone else. Knowing that God is *all* there is, he knows that this allness is right *where* he is, operating *through* what he is doing, manifesting itself through his word and in his act; that there is no difference between his thought of action and the action which is to proceed from that thought.

THE PRACTITIONER
SPEAKS WITH AUTHORITY

THE PRACTITIONER KNOWS THAT HIS WORD IS THE LAW OF
Mind in action, consciously neutralizing, obliterating or casting
out anything and everything that denies the perfect center. His
spiritual diagnosis reveals what is eternally true. The words he
uses have the power to dissipate that which denies this truth. He
speaks with an authority based on two fundamental propositions
which he has accepted.

The first one is the presence of pure Spirit in everything.
There is nothing in human logic to deny this assumption. There
is nothing in scientific discovery to refute it. The whole body of
individual and collective intuition throughout the ages gives it
validity. God really is all there is. This is more than a statement
of faith. It is a statement of cosmic fact. This first assumption, that
God is all there is and that pure Spirit exists in Its original form
everywhere, is the basis for all correct spiritual mind treatment,
no matter what the purpose of the treatment may be.

The second authority of the practitioner has grown up through the experience of an ever-increasing number of persons who have discovered that thought responds to thought, that a positive statement can and does neutralize a negative one. This second authority is not an assumption, it also is a reality.

The statements of the practitioner are spoken with calm assurance that nothing can obstruct the truth. This is not the authority of one mind exercising an influence over another, but rather, the authority of Truth Itself—just as one working in the field of physical science exercises authority through his knowledge of the laws of physics. He knows if he puts certain combinations together, they will produce inevitable results. The results will be both mathematical and mechanical. The spiritual mind practitioner uses the same authority. It is the authority of Law enforcing Itself.

Any belief that we lack the ability to use this Law rises from the mistaken idea that it is either our will or concentration which accomplishes the desired result. Quite the reverse is true. The result has nothing to do with will or concentration any more than it would have in physical science. The physicist neither wills nor concentrates. He uses the laws of nature. His concentration is merely the attention he gives to the conscious use of these laws. He does not try to hypnotize or influence anyone, nor does he hold thoughts over the laws of nature. He merely lets them work through the channels he has designated.

Let us shift this into the field of mental and spiritual law and follow the same method. There is a spiritual energy at the center of everyone and everything. There is no material or physical resistance to this energy any more than there is a resistance to the laws of nature. Any apparent resistance to the laws of nature is not in the laws but in the way we use them. This is true in spiritual mind practice—resistance is not in the Law of Being but in our attitude toward It.

The practitioner must have a complete conviction that there is no resistance to his word. It must be impossible for him to conceive of any such resistance. He cannot arrive at this conviction if he feels that his thought is manipulating persons and conditions. He can arrive at it only through a recognition that the spiritual laws of nature operate through his word and produce definite results. Everyone who has had faith through prayer has done this, but he has seldom done it consciously.

EXAMPLE

Because I believe in the power of God and know that the Law of good operates upon my word of faith, I speak this word with complete abandonment, I speak it with enthusiasm and joy. I speak it with a deep sense of calmness and peace. I know that I am governed by Divine Intelligence, that my word is a channel of inspiration through which guidance continually flows to me.

I am completely receptive to this guidance and live in a consciousness of joyful expectation of the good, acknowledging that God, around, in and through me, is the only power there is operating in all I do, say or think. I let this power direct me into constructive channels of self-expression.

Stated in its simplest terms, the spiritual practitioner, without denying the body, the environment or the physical world, seeks to bring them into line with a recognition of spiritual or divine realities. When he says, "God is all the presence, power and activity there is," he is not merely mumbling a lot of words; he is consciously bringing his thought, through faith and conviction, under the government of a superior harmony, a coordinating will, and a necessary Divine Presence.

This is not an act of superstition, nor is it a vain repetition of words or wishful thinking. The practitioner's mind is not in a dream state. Quite the reverse. It is more nearly like coming out of a dream state into a greater reality. It is neither a vain repetition of words nor is it wishful thinking for one to believe in the underlying unity of all life. It is the very essence of clear thinking. Every deep spiritual thinker who ever lived has believed this. It is not idle dreaming or wishful wishing when one declares that there is a Divine Pattern for this physical body. It is merely bringing his concept of body under the government of the Divine Harmony.

If this Divine Harmony and Unity did not exist, there would be no universe. Metaphysics is an unusually persistent and stubborn attempt to think straight. The whole endeavor of a spiritual mind practitioner is straight thinking. And to him, straight thinking means that his thought shall be based on the assumption that there is a coordinating Will, a spiritual Presence, a Divine Pattern and a universal Purposiveness in and throughout all nature, including man himself.

The practitioner should have a sense of the absoluteness of the Principle with which he deals, an uncompromising sense of the authority of spiritual Law. When Jesus said that a knowledge of the truth can make us free, he was stating this Principle. "It is I who speak unto you," that is, it is the Truth proclaiming Itself. He spoke with the authority and conviction of one who had seen through both the physical and the psychic life to that spiritual wholeness which exists at the center of every person's being, that Kingdom of God which is within.

Experience has proved that he was right. We now know that the spiritual practitioner may exercise such an authority; that he does so as he clarifies his own consciousness about his patient. His authority is not that of one who feels that he knows something that others could not know, or that he has been endowed with some grace of Providence which has been denied to others. His is the authority of one who knows there are spiritual and mental laws in the universe just as there are physical laws, and that they operate in the same manner. He believes in these laws and knows how to use them.

The spiritual mind practitioner does not think of himself as a healer any more than a mathematician thinks of himself as the principle of mathematics. There is but one healing agency, which is Life, Spirit or Truth. There is but one Life Principle, which is the Law of Mind in action; but one Spirit, which is God in everything.

The final law of life is a law of good. There is but one ultimate impulsion in the universe. This impulsion sis love. This love is more than an emotional sentiment, although it must include all such emotional sentiments. It is the pure essence of Divine Givingness.

There is something in the universe which forever gives itself to its creation, forever offers itself, not as a sacrifice, but as an impartation of its essence into everything. The practitioner must sense this Divine Givingness, this Divine Love, as the manifestation of Spirit through everything. He must sense the harmony of the Divine Life, which, should we permit It, could give such power to our thought that it would become irresistible as law, not through will or concentration, but by attention and willingness.

The highest laws of life cannot be profaned. It is only as we come into union with good that we have the power of good. Evil blocks itself, congests its own effort, dams its own stream and destroys its own purpose. Good cannot be blocked. Otherwise, the universe would destroy itself. We need never worry about the wrong use of spiritual power. There is no such thing.

The practitioner must have a calm which transcends any confusion he wishes to change. He must have a sense of justice which outweighs any manifestation of injustice. And he must have a sense of the immediate availability of good—not as though he were reaching out *toward* it, but rather, as though he were reaching out *with* it. As his thought blends with goodness it becomes a law of goodness. He does not make good out of evil. In the process of transformation the evil disappears while the good remains.

More and more we shall come to see that spiritual mind practice is not an assumption but a proclamation. In this practice the practitioner is rising above confusion and everything that contradicts the Divine Harmony, and he must so live and think that it is possible for him to do this.

Jesus said that the blind cannot lead the blind. There must be a seeing eye, a discerning consciousness, an inward awareness. The practitioner applies this inward awareness for a definite purpose. He is harnessing the energy and the activity of this awareness to a definite intention. The result will be as certain as his consciousness makes it because it will correspond with that consciousness.

It is in this sense that God is the answer to every human need. The Divine Spirit is the knower in us; the Universal Law is the actor. The savior is Christ in us, knowing through us. There is no opposite to this, nothing competes against it, nor can it be monopolized. All of God is everywhere present. The entire possibility of the action and reaction of the Law is ever available. Any result is merely a reflected image, never a thing in itself, always in the realm of effects projected by causes over which the conditions themselves have no control whatsoever. The conditions themselves automatically respond by corresponding.

We are accustomed to thinking that the Word of God is the

Law of God. We are not so used to thinking of our own word as the activity of this universal Presence and Law. We think of ourselves as separated from It rather than one with It. Therefore we feel that we have to reach out toward It, not realizing that It is not afar off but within. We go in search of that which we already possess but are not using.

The practitioner must discover the great Reality within himself. It is his consciousness of this Presence which gives power to his word. The principle he is using is the Law of Mind in action; the method for using it is conscious thought. It is the practitioner's business to combine his inward awareness with the conscious use of the Principle for definite purposes, for himself, for others, and for any condition which needs changing. Anyone who practices this will find proof of its reality. Thus alone can he know that he is dealing with certainty, with law, with love, and with life.

The practitioner speaks with authority, but it is not the authority of combativeness. Rather, it is the authority of a deep spiritual conviction. Should the practitioner feel that his authority is mind over matter, or good over evil, he will have a sense of combativeness, as though he were grappling with a real adversary. It is only as he views the adversary as shadow rather than substance that he exercises spiritual authority.

When he says, "I know there is but one Mind and one Power, which is God. I know I am one with all the good there is. I am conscious that what I know will remove doubt, fear and its manifestation," he speaks as one who, in calm contemplation, is merely saying to himself, "I am carrying a light into a darkened room and I know that as I carry this light the room will be illumined."

He is not combating the darkness, he is not treating it as though it were a thing in itself. He is thinking of it merely as a negative condition which will automatically be dissipated by the light. Perhaps it would be better for him to say, "There already is a light in this room but someone or something has placed a heavy shade before it. I will remove the shade. The light that was already there will now be revealed." These are merely suggested methods by which a practitioner clears up his consciousness.

His word is spoken with calm conviction and in deep trust, with absolute faith and assurance, but without heaviness. It is spoken from the consciousness of one who knows that the Divine Center already exists, and that he is merely revealing it. Spiritual treatment is the proclamation of a consciousness one has accumulated or gathered into himself as a result of much watching and waiting. It is a result of the deep communion of his mind with the spiritual universe.

EXAMPLE

If a practitioner were treating someone for greater self-expression, he would clarify his own consciousness by affirming:

Divine Mind is always present, always peaceful, calm and sure of Itself. It is always creating. What It creates is harmonious, happy and always brought to fruition. There is no discord in the Divine Intelligence. It sees things as complete and perfect.

He then directs his thought for his patient. He declares:

Divine Intelligence is directing him, thinking and knowing through him. The Law of Good, which is the Law of Mind in action, is now bringing everything in his life to fruition. This man not only knows what to do, he is impelled to do it. Everything in his life is brought under control of the law of harmony. There is no deferment, no delay, no obstruction or obstacle, nothing to impede the progress of right ideas. The doorway of opportunity and self-expression is always open. There is an increasing awareness of this in his mind and an increasing manifestation of it in his affairs.

The practitioner is doing two definite things in his own consciousness. First, he is arriving at a sense of the allness of Good, the ever-present activity of the Divine Mind. Next, he is declaring that this activity is flowing out into the affairs of the one he is working for.

A case is won or lost in the consciousness of the practitioner. Unless he knows this to be true he will limit the effect of his treatment to the conditions he wishes that treatment to change. This whole process of realization takes place within his own thought. The Law responds by corresponding to his consciousness. His use of that Law is entirely independent of any existing condition whatsoever. It makes things out of Itself.

Fact and concept are one and identical. They are the same thing. They are not separated by any sequence, nor interfered with by any external agency. The practitioner knows this. Inspired by spiritual conviction, he speaks his word in calm confidence, and the result will be as certain as is his faith.

It is said that Jesus spoke as one having authority. While others were amazed at his words, Jesus no doubt would have been more amazed had his word failed to fulfill itself. His assurance was a result of years of patient work with himself until finally his realization of Spirit was greater than other people's belief in the necessity of certain conditions.

Finally, every man must rely on his own consciousness, his immediate awareness of God, his authority in the Law. The world has mostly been superstitious about the Invisible, has waited for prophets, has depended upon saints and saviors. Without in any way detracting from the beauty of the lives of the saints, and using them as noble examples, we must still show people that they have an immediate and personal relationship with the Invisible. They must establish within themselves such a conscious union with good that they need no longer go in search after God.

True teaching liberates the student from his teacher. He will find the teacher within himself. This will not make him arrogant or egotistical; rather, he will have a deep sense of humility, as we all should when we face the great Reality. This humility is not self-deprecatory. It is the humility of one who is humble before the greatness of everything, even though he feels one with it. He knows that God is greater than he is; he also knows that he is in and one with God.

We should have a spirit of adventure in this—the wonder of it, the continual discovery, the steady unfoldment, the joyful anticipation of more and better, the silent recognition of our partnership with the Invisible. We should have a deep sense of calm and peace, an abiding faith and trust in the universe. This is the essence of faith, the beauty of religion.

SPIRITUAL CAUSE
AND PHYSICAL EFFECT

THE INFINITE MIND MUST BE MANIFEST. IT MUST MANIFEST Itself in persons, places and things. If the Infinite Mind were not active It would be unconscious. Everything in the manifest universe is a result of Its activity. It is this activity as its own effect.

In practicing the Science of Mind we do not deny the physical body nor the physical universe. Instead of denying the physical universe, we affirm that it is controlled and governed by a principle of harmony, of unity and of peace. It is necessary that Life clothe Itself in form, else It would remain unexpressed. Creation is a result of the self-knowingness of the creative Spirit. Consciousness clothes itself in form in the individual life as well as in the universal.

The physical body is not an illusion nor is it unreal, but it is an effect contained within something that projects and governs it. It is subject to this higher intelligence. We never deny the physical body or the physical organs. We affirm that body is a spiritual idea, that every organ, action and function must have a spiritual prototype or equivalent back of or within it. The practitioner affirms a body that is spiritual here and now, a body of right ideas, harmoniously adjusted to each other, functioning in accord with natural rhythm and harmony.

We are not creating a spiritual body but realizing that there must be one. Because we focus this realization for a definite purpose, the reaction will permit a more complete flow of spiritual life. The practitioner works in the realm of causes. The result of his work projects into the realm of effects. The effect will always equal its cause. It can never be more, less nor different. Thoughts are things and objective situations are the Law of Life experiencing Its own fulfillment. All action is the action of the Spirit in and upon Itself. There is nothing to inhibit this action.

In such degree as one is able to sense this he will have removed the obstructions to a true functioning of an organ. He will neither have created an organ nor its activity. He will have more clearly sensed that its action is in harmony with the rhythm of the universe.

It is a mistake to suppose that we must separate the physical body from its spiritual idea. Quite the reverse. We seek to unite the object with its subject, always realizing that the spiritual reality is present and active, here and now. This is true of everything, from a blade of grass to a solar system, from the movement of the tides to the movement of thought in our own consciousness. Everything that is, is a manifestation of one Life, which is always in harmonious accord with Its own nature. There is but one Cause. It is immediate in Its manifestation in and through everything. Spirit is the activity of everything—not separated or apart from Its manifestations, but in them.

Whenever there is anything wrong it is the endeavor of the

practitioner to transpose it, using the condition as a sign or a guide in the sense that no matter how negative it is, it is always a misinterpretation of truth. Illusion is not in conditions or things of themselves, but in the way we interpret them.

What the practitioner denies is not activity but wrong action. For instance, in thinking of the body, every organ, action and function must have a spiritual equivalent or reality to its nature. We do not say there is no liver. We say that liver is a spiritual idea or reality. The activity of this idea is present where we perceive or experience the physical liver. It is congestion, stagnation or inaction that we consider to be false. It is an experience, but a wrong one.

In doing this we are not claiming that there is a true and a false liver. From the standpoint of idealistic philosophy there is a universal idea of every organ. This universal idea is individual to each person. This is an abstraction, the logic of which we but dimly discern; its full meaning we seldom perceive.

In actual practice we permit logic or reason to carry us as far as it can and then boldly jump overboard into the ocean of our being. There is an intuition within us which always backs up such reason as we possess. When we state in a treatment that a Divine Idea is always active, we are not thinking of an activity which is external, but internal. Nothing can separate the activity of Spirit from an organ because the two are identical.

The practitioner realizes that there is but one Spirit or Life Essence in the universe; every manifestation is some form of this original source, and this source is centered in himself, as it is in everyone else. He proceeds on the basis that Mind, in its unformed state, and mind in form, are identical, that is, matter is mind in form. It derives its entire being from an invisible principle which is universally present, which, in its original state, permeates and penetrates everything. Intelligence, operating in this Mind Principle, produces form. The form always corresponds with the idea held in intelligence.

EXAMPLE

I know that as there is one Mind, that Mind is God and that Mind is my mind, so also there is one Body, that Body is spiritual and that Body is my body. So, every organ, every function, every action and reaction of my body is in harmony with the divine creative Spirit. I have both "the mind of Christ" and the Body of God.

I live in the one Mind and act through the one Body, in accord with divine harmony, perfection and poise. Every organ of my body moves in accord with perfect harmony. The Divine circulates through me automatically, spontaneously and perfectly. Every atom of my being is animated by the Divine Perfection.

My body, and every part of it, is made of pure substance—God. It cannot deteriorate. This instant this infinite substance within me, that is constantly flowing through me, takes form in the likeness of perfect, whole, complete cells. My body (Spirit in form) knows no time, knows no degree; it knows only to express fully, instantaneously. The perfect Life of God now expresses through me, and every part of my body expresses its innate perfection and wholeness.

Accompanying his technique, the practitioner must have a positive faith, a conviction, a complete acceptance of the spiritual universe, of spiritual man, here and now. No matter what the evidence to the contrary, the practitioner should not permit himself to judge according to its appearance.

The truth that man is a spiritual being now as much as he ever shall become, that the Kingdom of God is an accomplished fact, that the spiritual laws of life work automatically, that it is actually done unto us as we believe—these are the tools with which a practitioner works, silently meditating upon the good, upon peace and joy, upon the fullness of life, which he knows the Spirit must be, and identifying himself and his patient with that Life which is forever perfect.

Pure Spirit is at the center of every organ, action and function of man's being. It is not brought down into man's being through our statements. Rather, it is revealed by them. We are not trying to create a truth or a principle. We are endeavoring to perceive a truth. We are using a principle which automatically reacts to us by corresponding with our mental attitudes. Jesus affirmed this when he said, "It is done unto you as you believe."

Since the Law of Mind acts for us by corresponding with our mental attitudes it follows that action and reaction are automatic and equal. Everything that is, is a result of one universal Law acting and reacting upon Itself. The practitioner never feels that anything opposes his work. His endeavor is to keep his own consciousness in line with the affirmative side of life; therefore, his analysis, even of a negation, results in a conscious recognition of the exact opposite, which is the true affirmation about that situation.

In applying this principle to the healing of disease, the practitioner assumes that health is part of the eternal Reality. The spiritual man has no disease. The spiritual man represents pure ideas which are always operating. And it is the spiritual man he is talking about. There is no congestion, confusion, infection or wrong action in spiritual ideas. Pure ideas cannot be overactive, inactive or underactive. The action of Truth is continuous, vital, harmonious and perfect.

The practitioner declares this to be the truth about his patient and follows this declaration with all the spiritual realization he has, a feeling within him which says "Yes" to what his intellect affirms. The words used in treatment, the thoughts employed, are an affirmation of this inward awareness, this spiritual feeling the practitioner has. They are methods through which he states his conviction at any particular moment.

There is a feeling within everyone which responds to this, implanted by the Divine Mind Itself. The fact that we exist is a sufficient demonstration or proof of this assertion. We did not create our own being. Man has a spiritual existence, and because this is true, there is always an echo from his spiritual nature down into the intellect.

Since he believes that Spirit is at the center of everything, the practitioner draws no line between what can and cannot be helped through mental and spiritual work. So far as modern psychology is concerned, it is always stretching the line backward, anyway, and bringing more and more physical conditions into the realm of emotional causation. The metaphysician merely goes the whole way, announces that God is all there is, that the laws of the universe must of necessity be harmonious, and that there must be a spiritual body, whether or not he understands it.

The spiritual mind practitioner theoretically resolves everything into mind, feeling that mind in its invisible or liquid form is no different from mind in its objective or more solid shape; that the two are identical, and that when the stream of consciousness is changed about a condition, the condition must of necessity change to correspond with it. The practitioner transposes material facts into their spiritual correspondents and stays with the spiritual correspondent until the material fact surrenders its discordant image to a pattern more in accord with the Divine Nature.

70

ACTIVITY OF RIGHT IDEAS

IF WHAT GOD KNOWS HE KNOWS FOREVER, WOULD IT FOLLOW, then, that human activity, being the Divine Mind thinking and knowing through the human, must necessarily be permanent? The answer seems to be that we cannot limit the Infinite by saying It must forever do a certain thing in a certain way. While it is true that the nature of the Infinite cannot change, it seems equally certain that Its activity can never cease to change, any new change always being in accord with the fundamental harmony of Its being.

"Behold, I make all things new." There is nothing permanent but change and the Infinite Intelligence can never be caught in anything It does. What It does expresses Its being at that particular time. Tomorrow It may do it in an entirely different way, but always in accord with Its fundamental harmony.

It is necessary for us to see that unity does not mean uniformity and that the changeless nature of the original Mind in no

71

way imposes monotonous action upon It. Every moment is a fresh, new and spontaneous expression, and should be so considered. Therefore, we should always work for new ideas and they will always come.

When one conceives a new idea he is actually specializing the Law of cause and effect for the definite and specific purpose implied in the idea. He is specializing a Law, not creating It. The mental Law of cause and effect, like all other laws of nature, is a neutral, impersonal, creative force always operating mechanically and mathematically, always right where we are and ever ready and willing to respond. Intelligence operating in and through this Law sets It in motion for Creative purposes.

We are using this Law at all times, whether or not we are aware of the fact, and It is always responding. When we look at our environment and see many things that are not desirable, instead of thinking of them as conditions which fate has imposed upon us, we should recognize them as the orderly procession of the Law of cause and effect moving in logical sequence to definite form.

We should know that the impulsion in this Law was either consciously or unconsciously—and, of course, mostly unconsciously—caused by our own thinking or the thinking of the world. The Law of Mind cannot move unless ideas move in It, and things cannot be projected unless the Law projects them. The great cosmic order of the universe, which man did not create, is an outward picture of God's thought. In it we behold the Meditation of God, the Body of God, God seeing Himself in what He does.

What relationship does universal Intelligence have to individual activities? What is the relationship between Spirit and a man's business or profession? The Divine Mind, being the sole and only creative agency in the universe, finds in each individual a new and fresh starting point for Its action.

This is a conclusion which the deepest thinkers of the ages have arrived at. It in no way limits the infinity of Mind. It does show that in the Infinite there is neither big nor little. It is the cause of all action, even what we call large and small. Each thing is to It as an individual action of Itself; therefore, all the power, presence, activity and law there is, is back of every individual act.

When one writes it is the universal Mind calling on Its own creativeness to project an idea which It holds in Its own imagination. Emerson said that history can be understood only by realizing it to be an activity of the universal Mind on this planet through a period of perceptible time. The writing of a novel is just as much an activity of this Mind as the creation of a planet.

The way to work for an author is to know that Divine Intelligence is operating through his consciousness. The Mind of God is writing this novel. The one through whom It works can draw upon It for limitless characterizations. When Divine Intelligence makes a demand on Itself, It answers the demand in the terms of the demand made. Therefore, the writer making a demand upon himself is the Divine Mind waiting on Its own answer.

When we apply this principle for an author who cannot seem to work out the right plot for his play, or who seems to lack right characters or to know what to do with the ones he has, we must know that the Divine Mind cannot be confused. A demand has been made upon It and there is nothing between the demand made and Its flow through the consciousness of the individual being worked for.

The practitioner clears up his own thought until he knows that all the creative imagination in the universe is now welling up through the consciousness of this particular writer, operating intelligently, instantly, and without effort. He knows that every character ever created, anything and everything that any character would or should do under any circumstances, is known to Mind. The consciousness of the author is this Mind in action. There is nothing to obstruct Its passage. Words, thoughts and acts formulate and flow without effort through the consciousness of the writer. When this is done, originality will follow. No imitation will be necessary.

Originality means exactly what the word signifies—something unique, different, unlike anything else that ever was or ever shall be, the original Thinker thinking a new manifestation. This is the way the practitioner thinks of the one he is working for, and according to the clearness of his thought a demonstration will be made.

The same principle would apply in the running of a business, a profession or any activity one might be engaged in. There is no hard or easy, no great or small. The entire universe is an infinite Mind knowing Itself to be what It is and manifesting Itself in infinite variations.

EXAMPLE

I know that what (speaking the person's name) is doing is an activity of the Infinite Mind. It knows what to do under any and every circumstance; therefore, he knows what to do. It is knowing in him now, today. His business is the activity of this Mind in his personal affairs, at this particular time.

I know that the Spirit goes before him, making plain his way. Everything he does shall be prospered because he is in partnership with the Infinite. It is his desire that only good shall go from him, therefore, he has a right to expect that only good shall return to him. He lives under the government of Good and is guided by the Spirit of God. This I affirm. This I accept.

An active consciousness demonstrates spiritual understanding. This does not mean that the practitioner assumes the responsibility for the healing. What he assumes is the obligation to do his work earnestly, sincerely, and with deep conviction. His consciousness is active in knowing the spiritual truth about his patient. Through experience he has learned that the Law of Life responds to him by corresponding with his mental attitudes. The responsibility of the healing is in the principle he uses. The obligation to use the principle intelligently belongs to the practitioner.

He is mentally alert to detect whatever needs to be erased and to become actively engaged in contemplating its exact opposite—the truth he desires to see manifest. For instance, if he is treating someone for activity in his affairs, he specifically recognizes and definitely states that the activity of good is now surrounding the person or the condition he is working for. He is bringing his consciousness of activity to bear on a definite problem. The problem will be solved when the condition passes from inaction into action.

Suppose someone were to come to a practitioner, saying, "I don't know what to do. I have many things I might choose to do, but none is definite." The practitioner should work to know that the activity of Intelligence now flowing through this man's mind causes him to make correct decisions. Automatically, the confusion will clear up. He will make definite decisions and operate on them.

EXAMPLE

In the case of someone who feels he has missed previous Opportunity and thus become a failure, the practitioner affirms:

There is no thought of failure that can operate through this person's mind. He is open to the influx of new ideas, new thoughts and new opportunities. He recognizes and intelligently acts upon the opportunities presented to him. Every thought of not being wanted, or being afraid, every thought of uncertainty and doubt is cast out of his mind. His memory goes back to God alone, in whom he lives, moves and has his being.

I know that his consciousness and imagination are continually stimulated with new ideas, and he operates upon these ideas constructively and intelligently, with no sense of strain. A complete sense of happiness, peace and certainty floods him with light. He has confidence in himself because he has confidence in God. He is sure of himself because he is sure of God.

The whole treatment is built around the concept of the limitlessness of the God nature, the ever-increasing flow of good to yourself or the person you wish to help. The practitioner is not trying to make something happen, but rather, to realize that something is happening. He formulates his statements in such a way that if the words were actual things which immediately formed before him, the form would be desirable.

It is not at all necessary for a practitioner to know the specific details of the action that is to take place. It is necessary that he shall believe it does take place. If the practitioner feels that his patient is lacking in faith and confidence, he treats him to have faith and confidence. If he feels that his patient is vacillating and undecided, he treats to know that the patient knows what to do and acts on his knowledge. The practitioner is, as it were, pouring out a power for the one he is helping. The one being helped automatically distributes that power through the channels of his own awareness.

This explains why it is that although a practitioner gives practically the same treatment for activity in every case, the result is different for each person. If ten persons were to come to a practitioner asking for right action in their affairs, each would be different. Each would be individual. We might say that the practitioner pours a liquid substance over all their needs. It fills the need of each and flows back into itself. None of its energy is lost. But these ten people, each having brought his own bucket, will each carry away what his individual bucket holds.

If the buckets do not hold enough the practitioner should treat for an increased consciousness of substance, of activity, of happiness, or of whatever the need is. In this way the mental expectancy and acceptance of the patient is increased. His bucket will hold more, he can dip up more from the universal sea of good.

We can make bigger buckets. We cannot make a bigger law. The Law knows nothing about big and little. It knows to do. Since there is such a Law and we are always using It, we are all receiving from Life an objective equivalent of our inward mental attitudes. If we wish more we must increase our expectancy, we must identify ourselves with more. The Law, being absolute, can produce what we call a big thing as easily as what we term a small thing. Mind is a mirror, automatically reflecting our images of thought, be they good, bad or indifferent; large, medium or small, as we measure things.

EFFECT OF RACE THOUGHT

THE LAW OF MIND CAN KNOW THE INDIVIDUAL ONLY AS HE knows himself; otherwise, It would not be a law, It would be a person. It is upon the impersonality of the Law that the practitioner relies. But it must also be realized that the individual subconsciously knows or believes much about himself that contradicts his true spiritual nature.

The accumulated experience of the whole race is lodged in the subconscious of everyone and operates through everyone until a passageway is cleared back through the mind to the spiritual Presence which has never been affected by the race thought. While perfection is at the center of everything, the ages have built up a sense of disease and discord which has been transmitted from one person to another. It is lodged in the general race belief.

From this source, through unconscious suggestion, it passes into the life of the individual and more or less hypnotizes everyone from the cradle to the grave. It is the business of the practitioner to free thought from the bondage of this race suggestion.

In assuming this we are not departing from what is reasonable. The individual's subjective and unconscious reactions to life are largely drawn from the sum total of human experience. The subjective reactions of the individual are a result of personal experience, plus the collective experience, plus the impact of the universal Mind upon the consciousness of everything.

There seems to be a conflict between the original creative urge, its desire for self-expression, and the repressive action which has been brought to bear upon it. The Bible refers to this as the flesh warring with the Spirit. It also states that the Spirit will finally triumph over the flesh. Truth must finally triumph over error.

This collective thought has been called the mortal mind, the human mind, the carnal mind, race suggestion, or the collective unconscious. We should not become confused over terms, but learn to simplify their meaning and find the most direct approach to that meaning.

Taking such facts as we know to be true, we arrive at the conclusion that the whole race experience has created a collective field of thought and belief, which seeks to operate through everyone. Let us add another idea—which is accepted by most workers in this field—that morbid thought patterns tend monotonously to repeat themselves over and over through life. This is true of collective thought patterns as well as individual ones.

It makes no difference whether this collective thinking takes the form of believing that the mistakes of our forefathers are visited on us, or whether, believing in previous births, we think our own karmic law inflicts a bondage on us; both are equally fallacious. When Jesus healed a certain man who was born blind, he disproved both propositions.

Because everyone is an individual and cannot wait until the collective unconscious of the whole race is cleared up, everyone must break down the barriers which tie him to the race belief. In so doing he will not only be healing himself of the mesmeric effect of race thought, he will also be contributing to the final redemption of the whole race.

This is why it is that we start with the proposition that evil of any nature or anything that contradicts the supremacy of good, the all-conquering power of love and the immediate availability of God, are blocks in consciousness and must be removed. Evil does not belong to anyone. It is merely a heritage of the ages believed in by so many persons that it seems to be true.

The practitioner knows that there is but one Law of Mind in action. When, in treating a patient, he is confronted with discord or inharmony, he treats it merely as a negative thought force operating through the patient. It does not belong to him at all. It is no part of his spiritual nature. It is human experience repeating itself in this individual. It is operating from the subconscious reaction of the whole race. It is a false suggestion acting as though it were true. He removes this suggestion by a contradiction of it, through a denial of it, and by a realization of its opposite.

For instance, the truth about hate is love. Hate is merely a negative assertion of love. To the practitioner, hate is not a law, not a person, not a place, not a thing. It is a state of consciousness which has found entrance to someone's mentality. Love consumes hate by its presence just as light overcomes darkness. Love is the positive statement about hate. Hate is a negation of love, its denial, unfounded in any basic reality. The practitioner separates the belief from the believer.

81

Even in psychological practice this is held to be true because everyone working in this field knows that he must separate the neurosis from the neurotic. How could he do this unless he assumed an ego or person who is not subject to the neurosis or the false claim, as we would call it? He could not.

The proposition is equal to one accepted on the physical plane when we affirm that the way to light a dark room is to introduce a light. If the darkness had power over the light, if it were anything other than a condition, then it might refuse to give up its place. It might, if it were an entity, for instance, say, "I am darkness. I persist in remaining darkness. I know only darkness. I believe only in darkness. This is what I am and this is what I remain. Nothing can resist me." But the darkness cannot do this. It is a condition instantly dissipated in such degree as light is introduced.

In spiritual mind practice one accustoms himself to the idea that negative thoughts and conditions are not entities. They are but temporary disturbances in the mind. They are attached to the individual mind only in such degree as there is something in his consciousness which unwittingly holds them there. This whole process takes place in the field of what is called the unconscious or the subjective, and is probably unknown, unrecognized and unbelieved in by the conscious thinking of the one affected by it.

The practitioner knows that a negative condition cannot resist the truth, just as darkness cannot resist light. He does not contend against the negative condition. He practices spiritual non-resistance in the sense that he knows the absolute unreality, from the standpoint of Spirit, of discord. It is but a negative statement of the truth.

Whether one chooses to call it a thought pattern, a false belief, or a concealed error, makes no difference. These are but different terms used to describe an actual condition. Negative thought patterns do attach themselves to people, either as a result of their own previous experience, or, as we believe, more largely from the entire experience of the race itself.

It is in this sense that the practitioner in this field resolves all negation into mental attitudes; that he understands that mental negation and its experience are identical, they are not two things. The practitioner views the thought and thing as one and identical, which it is. It is only on this basis that he could change the thing by reversing the thought. Since thought and condition are one, when the thought is reversed the Condition automatically disappears.

The practitioner in spiritual mind science separates the belief from the believer just as the psychologist separates the neurosis from the neurotic. The practitioner reverses the thought patterns just as the psychologist resolves the conflict. If successful, the end result is more or less identical, with the great and fundamental exception that in spiritual mind practice the separation of the belief from the believer is of minor importance compared to the identification of the individual with the center and source of his being, which is pure Spirit.

EXAMPLE
I release all thought of fear from my mind. I lay down the burden of carrying the load of responsibility for life for myself or for others. I lay all trouble aside, seeking to look through it, beyond it, above it; to detach it from the realm of Reality, to separate it from any consciousness that it belongs to me or to anyone else, regardless of what any problem of the moment seems to be.

The practitioner then directs his thought for his patient:
I know that this man now realizes that fear is a lie, a fraud, since it

83

contradicts the Divine Presence, repudiates limitless Love and denies infinite Good. He is aware that it is neither person, place nor thing; it is merely an impostor that he has believed in.

Today he repudiates all fear. He renounces the belief in evil. He enters into conscious union ‑with the Spirit. He accepts the good as supreme, positive and absolute.

I know that every negative condition of the past is cleared away from his consciousness. He no longer thinks about it, sees it, or believes in it. Nor does he believe that it has any effect whatsoever in his experience. With joy he enters into the activities of the day; without regret he remembers the events of yesterday, and with confidence he looks forward to tomorrow, for today his heart is without fear.

He allows the Divine Wholeness to flow through him into ever-widening fields of activity. Every good which he has ever experienced is now increased ten fold. Every joy which he has ever experienced is now multiplied. There is a new influx of inspiration into his thought. He is conscious that his divine birthright is freedom, joy and eternal goodness. The Divine Presence interprets Itself to him in love and friendship, peace and joy, now and forever.

We should know that the consciousness of good acts as a law of right action. A consciousness of good, as it increases, always produces new and better circumstances in one's environment. There is no inertia of human thought, no morbidity of race consciousness, and no hypnotic grip of race suggestion. No one need be bound by the limitations human experience has set. They are always false. Every new horizon provides a fresh starting point for another horizon that is pushed even farther away. Progress is eternal, unfoldment is everlasting.

Since we are dealing with an infinite potential there can be no limit to its possibility. One should always be alert to this recognition. From the standpoint of Infinite Mind each day is a fresh beginning, every day is the world made new. We stand at the threshold of limitless possibility, of endless opportunity for self-expression. Every doorway is open, nothing inhibits or prohibits.

If the suggestion comes that this is too good to be true, we should treat it merely as the inertia of human thought itself declaring that we have gone as far as we can. The practitioner must recognize this argument as false. It is nothing claiming to be something. It is a lie claiming to be the truth. It is a habit pattern of thought unwilling to surrender itself. Should we let it, it will repeat itself with monotonous regularity throughout our lives.

On the other hand, should we concede that the possibility of our demonstration rests on anything that has gone before, either in our individual or collective experience, we shall limit the power of our word to the conditions imposed upon it by the consensus of human belief now operating through us as a law of our individual experience.

Here is a place where we may prove that the inertia of human thought patterns, seeking endlessly to recreate previous experiences, are but echoes of that greater possibility, which, instead of endlessly recreating previous experiences, may, with equal power, create new ones. If we concede that we can go thus far and no farther, we bind the limitless to our personal concepts, or, more truly stated, we bind our use of it to our accepted thought patterns. It is these thought patterns that we must break down.

We have created certain laws of limitation, or they have been created for us by the race, and unless we keep them in a fluid state in consciousness they can easily become obstructions to our progress. Keeping them in a fluid state in our consciousness, we can cause them to flow out as easily as they flowed in.

There is no actual resistance of thought patterns themselves other than the resistance of human consent; therefore, even this resistance is mental. It is never physical, it is never spiritual, it is always mental. If the obstruction is in consciousness, we can remove it through an act of consciousness. If it is a thing in itself, there is nothing we can do about it.

The practitioner knows that all obstructions are consciousness operating as temporary law. By reversal of these states of consciousness he clears the mental field and permits the Divine Creativity to flow fresh and new. It knows nothing about obstructions or obstacles or conditions, as such. It only knows Itself and Its knowing automatically creates the law of Its action.

In practice our whole proposition is whether or not we can see through the obstruction to the unobstructed field. This is why Jesus told us not to judge according to appearances. He did not say the appearances were false. He said, don't be hypnotized by them. Mental denial removes these obstructions and reverses the thought force that creates them, transmuting it into something else. Mental affirmation readjusts consciousness to a new influx of Life, while spiritual realization opens the floodgates of consciousness and lets through that which knows only the joy of its own self-expression.

If you are working for someone who needs to reorganize his life, his business or profession, work to know that nothing that has transpired can act as an obstruction, nothing that the race has ever believed can inhibit his action, nothing that all people combined have ever experienced can in any way hinder the flow of the original Mind through his consciousness.

Through such statements as these you are actually removing obstructions and freeing his consciousness to new creativity. A new faith and hope will come to him and an enthusiastic zest in living. Having removed the obstructions you now declare that new ideas are flowing through him, that he is impelled to see, understand, accept and act upon them. You are declaring that everything this man does must prosper because God's business is always prosperous, it is always good, it is always divinely organized and harmoniously executed.

Experience will accustom the practitioner to accept that positive statements actually clear consciousness of negative beliefs which have lulled it to sleep, have hypnotized it into accepting the dictates of the inertia of habitual thought patterns that always seek to perpetuate themselves. Jesus said to them: Sleep on and take your rest. I go into the garden that I may be alone with the original Cause. I surrender all inertia to this divine event. I resurrect my consciousness. I lift myself above this hypnosis.

Somewhere along the line we shall be compelled to do this. Every man must go into the garden of his own soul, and, lifting up his consciousness to the Divine Nature, find himself resurrected into a new life and a new light. In actual practice we do this every time we give a treatment. How could we do this if we believed that evil, lack, fear or any other negation is a law unto itself? We could not.

SUBJECTIVE
THOUGHT PATTERNS

JESUS TOLD HIS FOLLOWERS THAT WHEN THEY PRAYED THEY should believe their prayers were answered. This was a veiled statement of the Law of cause and effect. This Law operates on our beliefs as we believe them—not as we hope them to be, but as we actually believe them to be. If one has a clear belief in spiritual power, no matter what the appearance to the contrary may be, he can calmly state this belief as a present reality.

Suppose, in theory, we could arrive at this conclusion: man is born of pure Spirit through the avenue of human parentage. This is the way Divine Intelligence works. Like everything else which nature has done, we are compelled to accept the facts and go on from there.

Man has been endowed with a creative mind, whether or not he knows it. His belief or disbelief has nothing to do with it whatsoever. Even though he is born in a state of spiritual perfection, because he has a creative mind and because he is an

89

individual, he can think independently of the fundamental harmony in the universe. And because his thought is creative, it is always tending to build up situations and conditions in his body and environment which correspond to the unconscious patterns of his thinking.

The subjective state of one's thought—which means the sum total of his thought patterns—acts as a continual medium between the Absolute and the relative, between absolute and unconditioned Causation and the things that are happening in his everyday life.

These unconscious thought patterns, which are subjective, come from his environment, his everyday thinking, and from what the whole world believes. There are other patterns of thought which come from the deeper or spiritual side of his nature. The original patterns are in the Mind of God. A conflict arises between the impulsions of these original patterns and the repulsions of his conscious and unconscious thinking. This is the basis of mental conflict.

We now know that unconscious mental patterns repeat themselves with monotonous regularity. We see, then, that man is a house divided against itself. In his hope he exclaims, "I believe!" while something which seems to have almost equal power within him says, "You dare not believe." In his high moments of spiritual exaltation he says, "God is all there is," while something within says, "Maybe so. But just look about you!" And so the argument for and against life goes on automatically.

In the metaphysical field this has been called the "argument of error." In the psychological field it has been called the "inertia of thought patterns." In the metaphysical field, when these thought patterns are changed, there is an inner tearing or rending of them, as though they were being uprooted and pulled out against their will. This process has been called "chemicalization." In the psychological field it has been called "catharsis." In the Bible it was called "casting out devils."

In the metaphysical field it has been said that these habit patterns of thought do not like to give themselves up; they argue back, as when one says, "I believe," and then something within him says, "How can you believe?" In the psychological field this has been called the "resistance."

Putting these two generalized concepts together, and accepting that years of patient effort in both fields have exposed certain definite truths about the Law of Mind in action, we arrive at the conclusion that unconscious thought patterns do offer a resistance to conscious control, that they do actually set themselves up as though they were independent entities.

In the metaphysical field uprooting them has been called "uncovering the error." In the psychological field it has been called "resolving the conflict." In the psychological method the patient talks to the practitioner until, through the association of one idea with another, he gradually brings "to the light of day" the specific reasons for his conflict. The psychologist believes that the inner conflict must be dragged up and looked at by the conscious mind. The metaphysician knows he can resolve it in his own consciousness. In the metaphysical field this has been called "coming to know the Truth which frees us from error."

The analytical method is logical enough when we realize that it is based on the idea that there are many individual minds. The metaphysical method is also logical when we realize that it is based on the concept of one Mind Principle which many persons individualize or use. If there are many minds, then the individual mind affected must be individually analyzed and each block be brought to the surface and discharged. Because of this the process is long. On the other hand, if we assume but one

Mind Principle operating through everyone, we shall see that a practitioner removing a block in his own consciousness will at the same time be removing it from the consciousness of his patient.

In the metaphysical field it is not necessary that the practitioner shall know, or that the patient shall consciously know, what first induced these inward conflicts. The metaphysician has learned that by taking certain broad, generalized statements and realizing their meaning, conscious thought, acting as law, can and does remove the obstruction.

When this obstruction is removed, the metaphysician calls it "leaving the field to God." The psychologist calls it "coming to self-awareness" or "becoming adjusted to life." They have the same meaning. Because one field has held the other under suspicion, the similarities that exist have been lost sight of.

The metaphysician starts with the assumption that God or Spirit is the cause of everything. The psychologist is gradually coming to see this, and from now on we may expect to find a gradual concurring in the field of psychology with the need of a spiritual outlook on life.

It is self-evident that we came out of Life, God, Spirit, or whatever we choose to call the First Cause. We were placed here by an Intelligence superior to our intellects. The deepest thinkers of the ages have proclaimed that there is a divine pattern or prototype in the world of Spirit for everything that is projected into the world of created form. This pattern or prototype is not back of or outside its physical manifestation; it is at the center of it.

The spiritual mind practitioner starts with the bold assumption that man is a spiritual being now—not that he is going to become one or evolve into one. He is that. If everything that denies this can be removed, the divine pattern will come to the surface, the spontaneous flow of the original Cause will manifest itself in harmony, in peace and in wholeness.

We should realize that the Spirit continues to know through us. When our thoughts are based on the fundamental harmony it will begin to appear in our thinking. God is thinking the activity of our lives into definite expression through us right now. Our act of thinking or knowing, when it is based on this fundamental harmony, is just as much an act of the creative Mind of God as is speaking the physical universe into being.

If there is but one Mind to give birth to ideas, then God goes forth anew into creation through every man's life. The idea of shoes did not exist forever in the Mind of God, but the potential possibility was always there. The individual mind, feeling a need for shoes, conceives an idea, gives birth to a pattern, and the pattern gives birth to the object.

The Law through which this takes place already exists. The substance which passes into form already exists. The Divine Mind which conceives all ideas already exists. This Mind *is* the mind of man. He is an individual in It and uses It. It is the Mind through which he thinks. The original Law is always acting upon his thought, or his thought is acting through the Law—no one knows which. No matter which way we state the proposition, it amounts to the same thing.

The Law forever exists, the individual choice is a spontaneous thing. When it was discovered that nylon thread could be made of coal, air, water and other things in a mysterious combination, man was not creating either law or substance. But he was projecting an original pattern.

Did this original pattern already exist in the Divine Mind? No, this particular pattern did not exist. The potential possibility of it existed. Had someone else conceived the same idea a million years ago, the same pattern would have been created.

The pattern for nylon thread, or the formula, was a spontaneous emergence of the Divine Mind through an individual. It was a new creation.

In a way which we do not understand thoughts become things just as seeds become plants, just as a combination of coal, air and water turns into a physical substance from which yarn is made for the spinning of nylon stockings. In some way we do not understand, which is the mystery and miracle of Life, thoughts and mental attitudes become things.

Since this is true, ideas may be conceived of as possessing actual substance, operating through definite law, tending to produce specific form. The idea flows out of potential intelligence. It flows through ultimate substance. The intelligence is one, universally present and equally distributed. The substance is one, universally present and equally distributed. Whether we choose to call it the ethers of mind or the ethers of space or just the infinite possibility, makes no difference. The only significance names have is that they give meaning to ideas.

We did not create this universal order nor project this universal effect. Each one is, however, an individual center in it. He does project his relationship to it, which may or may not be one of adjustment, happiness and success. He also projects his individual use of it in his immediate personal life, and the union of all people's thought, or the majority of the consensus of human opinion, projects human history.

It is important for us to understand this and to realize the difference between projecting individual experience and human history and the projection of the universal order itself. In the moments of greatest human tragedy, individually or collectively experienced, nothing in nature is changed. The integrity of the universe is not violated nor the will of truth disturbed. The fundamental harmony, beauty, love and wisdom of the universe are not violated. The grass is still green, water is still wet, the sun still shines. As the great Master said, the rain still falls on the just and the unjust.

It is this original and fundamental harmony on which the practitioner in the science of spiritual mind healing relies. He knows that the original patterns must be perfect and harmonious, that the God-intended destiny must be happy and fruitful. But man, because of his free will, has disrupted his individual and collective life.

Everything that is of the nature of evil or discord has been created by man. The healing of all this must come through a reversal of thought and act, through bringing everything in man's life under dominion of the universal will and purpose, which must be truth, beauty, love, law and order, and fruitful and happy self-expression.

The universal Power is surrendered to the individual life only on the terms of Its own nature. No one can violate It. Real spiritual power is delivered only in such degree as one's mind is attuned to its fundamental harmony. No one can use real spiritual power for an evil purpose. It Is both unthinkable and impossible. We need not bother our minds with the query as to whether or not this can be done.

No one can make death out of life, or evil out of good, or hell out of heaven. But any man can so attune himself to good that his words become an instrument of its operation. It is then that he is thinking God's thoughts after Him. It is then that, through faith and understanding, he may proclaim the allness of the word he speaks, knowing that there is nothing in the universe to contradict his statement.

Let us see exactly how this works out in actual practice. Someone comes to a practitioner and says, "I am a lonely person. I do not make friends easily. I long for companionship and a close contact with human beings, but somehow or other I never seem to find the fulfillment of this, my deepest desire."

The Divine Creative Spirit has not ordained that certain persons shall become intimate friends of this individual. But the Divine Being, by Its very nature, has ordained that we all live, move and have our being in one, undivided, pure Spirit, which is Infinite Person flowing through innumerable personalities. While each person is a little different, because everything in the universe is individualized, at the base all are rooted in the Infinite Being. There is a place in every man's being where he is one with all that is because he is one with the universal Spirit which is in all that is.

The practitioner explains this to his patient. He tells him how to think. He points out to him that whenever thoughts of separation come into his mind he must supplant them with thoughts of union. He heals him of the belief in sensitiveness, and in his own mind the practitioner affirms the unity of all life and states that his patient is some part of this allness; he is forever one with the Spirit, consequently, he is forever one with all people.

The practitioner, being trained in conscious use of mental law, definitely and deliberately separates every belief in isolation, breaks down every affirmation of isolation, declares that his patient is now one with everyone whom he shall ever meet, that his life flows into and through all other lives without barrier, that he irresistibly draws into the orbit of his personal experience all people, things and conditions that make for the fulfillment of a happy, radiant and harmonious life.

EXAMPLE

This man no longer rejects himself. Knowing that he is one with all people in the Spirit, he receives everyone as a friend. He establishes a close and intimate relationship with everyone he meets—something goes out from him and becomes unified with them. He includes all and excludes none. He gives himself unstintingly to Life, unloosing the well-springs of his being spontaneously and with joy, withholding nothing. He does this with no thought of reward, but in the glad acknowledgment of this opportunity to increase his own livingness.

Higher than all differences is the union of the soul with its Source. Beyond all differentiation, the Infinite Person is enshrined in the sanctuary of his own consciousness. He is conscious of his union with all people, and he now enjoys this divine companionship. He embraces the Infinite in everyone and in turn is embraced by It.

As a result of this the Law of Mind will attract to this person those who can be made happy through his companionship. The basis of the treatment is a realization of the universal Presence. The realization of the universal Presence is now specialized through an equal realization of the union of this particular person with all other people. The divine pattern of union now flows out through this individual's experience and unites him with people.

Practice alone can verify these statements. No one ever practiced them actively without demonstrating their truth. We might say that the practitioner enjoys an inward sense of complete partnership with the universe. This is his secret, or the secret place of the most High within him. He understands that everything is governed by Law and that all laws must be the operation of Intelligence within Itself and upon Itself. He knows that wherever he designates a specific thing, place, person or condition, he is focusing a new use of the Law of cause and effect that will operate through that particular person, place or condition.

TIME ELEMENT
IN TREATMENT

THE PRACTITIONER IS ALWAYS FUNCTIONING IN THE PRESENT. The Spirit is a present reality. In every individual treatment the practitioner should know that the action of Truth is immediate, that everything in the nature of time, as we understand it, is eliminated. Every treatment must incorporate a consciousness of completion, of perfection and fulfillment, here and now.

If our consciousness functions only in a future state it automatically delays right action. Therefore, all statements are made in the present tense, all recognition in the here and now, all affirmations are acceptance, not of what is going to be, but of what now is.

When you treat someone the result of your knowing produces a corresponding knowing in his consciousness. A spiritual mind treatment is an active thing when it is given for a definite purpose. One should always be aware of the activity of ideas operating to definite ends. In such degree as the consciousness of a practitioner couples knowing with acting, through the realization that consciousness and action are identical, objective action will flow out of his words. The movement of the treatment is to this definite and specific end.

If activity does not follow, the practitioner will know that his work is not being done correctly, or that he must continue until right action does take place. Spiritual mind practice is not lulling oneself to sleep through an attitude of complacency. Right objective action will always follow right subjective action. The two are one and identical, they are two ends of the same thing. One is an image, the other a reflection of this image mirrored in experience.

Wherever there is inertia in experience there is inertia in consciousness. Wherever there is stagnation in the objective life there is equal stagnation in the subjective life. There is never any stagnation in the Spirit. Spiritual mind practice is not a method through which one becomes reconciled to the inevitability of unfortunate circumstances. It is quite the opposite. It awakens one to the realization that negative circumstances need not exist. One who feels that God will give us the grace to stand blows is not properly practicing this science.

The inertia of belief and the morbidity of experience have created such deep-seated thought patterns of negation that many sincere persons believe that through negative experiences they are gradually being led to the light. While this may be true in a sense, it would certainly be a negative basis for practice. God is not a failure, God is not sick, the Spirit is not limited, and Love has never learned anything by hate.

The practitioner should expect his first treatment to meet the case, while, at the same time, never taking "No" for an answer. If the first treatment does not meet the case, he must continue until a demonstration is made. But this question might arise: If one is dealing with a Principle which can instantly change any condition to a more desirable one, why should not any situation be instantly met?

Theoretically, there is no reason why the first treatment should not meet any situation, provided there is a complete realization, because realization and accomplishment are one and identical. The question is whether or not one has gained a complete realization in one treatment. The proposition could be stated in this way: there is but one treatment to be given, whether it takes ten minutes or ten months. If and when the treatment is complete, a demonstration will be made.

While it is necessary that expectancy and acceptance be woven into every treatment, it is also necessary to continue treatments until the desired result is obtained. The practitioner must train himself to come to a complete conviction in every specific treatment, and then forget that treatment. When he finds it necessary to repeat the treatment, he should not feel that he is continuing a process that is going to take a long time to accomplish, but that he is again stating the truth in as perfect a manner as possible.

Suppose we view each period of working as part of the whole treatment, some part of gaining a complete realization, knowing that when the realization is complete the demonstration will be made. Each period of giving this treatment, then, should last until there is the greatest possible degree of realization at that particular time, until a sense of agreement and assurance comes into the consciousness of the one giving the treatment. He feels that what he has said is true—it is the Truth about himself, about everyone, and particularly about the person he is working for, because he is specializing his treatment for this particular person or for some definite condition.

Perhaps it has taken him fifteen minutes, possibly it may have taken him thirty minutes, or even an hour, to arrive at this complete conviction. He has done everything he knows how to do in this particular treatment. He has reached a place of assurance and acceptance in his own consciousness. He believes that what he has said is the Truth. There is now no difference between knowing this Truth and its manifestation. He rests in the quiet assurance that all is well. He has a sense of ease and peace. He lets go of his treatment.

Each treatment is a specialized use of the Law of Mind for a particular purpose. The treatment exists for the fulfillment of that particular purpose. It has no intention and no action other than for the person mentioned and in the manner decreed. Each treatment has within itself the full capacity to execute itself at the level of the inward awareness of the one who gives it, for the purpose, person or thing specified in the treatment which he gives. Therefore, every treatment should be complete within itself.

No matter how many treatments one finds it necessary to give, each treatment must be complete. There must be a sense of finality about it. There must be a conviction that this is it, that it is done now—complete, perfect, finished. This consciousness should be in every treatment.

If it becomes necessary to take up the treatment again later in the day, the next day, or over a period of time, the practitioner continues in the same manner. Finally everything that inhibits the light of the Spirit from shining through will have been cleared away. He must be willing to continue treatment until the demonstration is made. While it is true that a demonstration should be instantaneous, it is also true that in the majority of cases the results are gained a step at a time, each period of realization bringing the consciousness a little nearer the goal.

There is no question but there are greater subjective blocks in some situations than in others, but that at the center of all manifestation there is a perfect life. Spiritual mind practice is the recognition of this perfect life, the acknowledgment of it, a realization of its meaning, an acceptance of its presence and action at the point of one's attention, whether this point be the physical body or any situation whatsoever.

Any individual treatment is incomplete until the one giving it accepts the verdict as present, final and perfect. This should be done in each individual treatment or the one giving it might fall into the habit of unconsciously deferring the outcome. In practice, then, each treatment is final. Persistence in spiritual work is necessary as in other fields. Flexibility and patience are necessary. This flexibility and patience are with one's own consciousness, not with the Principle he is demonstrating.

He may always have this assurance, that when his affirmation is complete, the answer will exactly correspond with it. Always the treatment is as effective as is the consciousness back of it. Consciousness can be changed, Reality cannot be. Therefore, if the practitioner is continually building up his consciousness he will progressively be revealing the Reality that underlies all things.

EXAMPLE

I align myself with the powers of goodness and of right action. I abide in perfect and complete faith in God as my ever-present good. I turn from all fear; turn joyfully and resolutely to faith, realizing that light is immune to darkness, that the night has no power over the day, that dawn dissipates the shadows of midnight. I turn my attention to the Light Eternal, without struggle, realizing that that Light, shining through the dark places of my consciousness, will dissipate them and that I shall walk in that Light in which there is no darkness.

Not only shall I walk in this Light, I shall radiate it. I shall impart it to others. I shall remember the saying, "Let your light so shine before men that they, seeing your good works, shall glorify your Father which is in heaven." I shall remember that the Father which is in heaven is in that heaven which is within me.

No person can successfully practice in this field beyond the point of merely mitigating evils unless he is willing to throw down the spiritual gauntlet to all evil and boldly assert that it does not belong to the province of good. God is not a becoming God. God is not an evolving God. God is that which was, is, and will remain perfect, complete, happy and harmonious.

This is the basis for all spiritual mind practice and the one who compromises with this position will accomplish but little in this field. But the pessimist will say, "Who, even among spiritual mind practitioners, has walked on the water or raised the dead or fed the multitude?" No person is spiritually equipped to practice this science who listens to such arguments. They arise from the inertia of human thought patterns which do not wish to be disturbed. They, too, would sleep on and take their rest. What if you haven't walked on the water or raised the dead? Perhaps you have made a good demonstration if you got passage on a boat to your destination or through objective methods found some way of feeding yourself with less anxiety.

Often a practitioner is confronted by so much confusion that his own mind may become disturbed. This, however, should not be considered a discouraging situation. It is merely an indication that more work is necessary for him to straighten out his thinking about this particular condition. It may even take him some time to do this. If he is a scientific practitioner, if he knows what he is doing and how to do it, he will continue until his entire consciousness responds from an inward sense of harmony.

The spiritual mind practitioner must ever be on the alert,

keeping his consciousness above what he sees, reads or hears. As increasing numbers of people do this, the human thought patterns of fear and limitation will gradually vanish. New and better ones will take their place, and finally, humanity itself will find a fresh starting point.

Everyone in this field should reserve portions of his time for deep spiritual meditation. The upper part of his mind must be kept in a listening attitude toward the Infinite that he may become a transmitter of peace from the eternal reservoir of Life to external things and events and to those whom he seeks to help. He must ever seek to be spiritually alert, always keeping some part of himself in a listening attitude toward Life that his consciousness may become a transmitter of that which is beyond human thought.

Let us assume a case where the patient says that he has always been bound by limitation. It is as though he were bound by a chain of negative causation from which he cannot extricate himself. He is thinking from the standpoint of previous experience. We cannot convince him that he has not had this experience, since he knows very well that he has. Merely the cold statement that nothing is wrong with him will not be effective. While it is true that nothing is wrong with the Spirit, it is also true that he is suffering from negative conditions, from lack and limitation.

It is not enough merely to say that all he needs is a change of consciousness. While this is a true statement, the statement itself will not change his consciousness. It would be like going into a room where everything is in the wrong place and saying, "Divine Harmony alone is real. The room is in a state of confusion because the people who have been living here are confused." This may be true enough, but the good housekeeper, seeing the confusion, will rearrange the furniture.

So it is with the spiritual mind practitioner. He does not meet a case by cold statements which merely reiterate that God is good. It is his business to *demonstrate* the truth of his statements. Therefore, he begins a systematic method of spiritual mind treatment which clears away the obstructions in consciousness and leaves the Spirit free to operate through his patient in a harmonious manner.

He might proceed as follows, always remembering that there are no formulas but that certain methods of procedure produce certain results.

EXAMPLE

Thinking of his patient, and knowing that his word is for this particular person, he might say:

The Spirit has no past. It has never been bound by any external conditions. It always has been, and forever will remain, free and independent of conditions. This man is of the essence of pure Spirit. He is one with God. I know there is no limitation operating in, around or through him. There is no burden of race belief obstructing him.

It makes no difference what happened yesterday, or what has happened in the past of this individual or the whole race. My word is a law of elimination to all beliefs and obstructions, no matter where they come from. This person is not bound by anything that has ever happened. The Spirit is creating everything new in his life today. He is free and unfettered. He dwells in the secret place of the most High. There is no fear, no uncertainty, no hesitation, no doubt.

Everything that he does shall prosper. The doorway of opportunity is open before him today. Everything that he does, says and thinks is stimulated by Divine Intelligence, impulsed by Divine Love. He is guided, directed and guarded into right action. Today, goodness, abundance, happiness, joy, success and friendship are increasingly made manifest in his experience.

The practitioner dwells on the meaning of these words. He seeks to realize the essence of their meaning. He feels his way back to that wholeness which exists at the center of all things. His words announce the activity of the Law of good, the Principle of Mind in action. He convinces himself of the words he speaks, and because he has directed this word for a particular person, it will manifest as soon as the words are spoken. It will continue to manifest unless the action of these words is denied.

RELATIONSHIP OF
PRACTITIONER TO PATIENT

THE SPIRIT OF BOTH THE PATIENT AND THE PRACTITIONER IS God, the One Spirit. This is why Jesus said that we should not judge others because if we do we shall be judged by the same judgment—"Judge not that ye be not judged, for with what judgment ye judge ye shall be judged, and with what measure ye mete it shall be measured to you again."

This goes beyond charity and tolerance. It strikes at the center of Reality itself. Only in a spirit of love, understanding and unity can there be wholeness. The practitioner identifies both himself and his patient with pure Spirit, refusing to admit any detachment from this Spirit either in himself or in his patient. Love is the great healing power—a love which sees through human errors to that Infinite which knows nothing outside Itself, nothing different from Itself, nothing other than Itself.

Always we shall see that spiritual mind practice is a combination of love and law—love as impulsion, law as propulsion. It is through love that we arrive at a sense of union. The slightest block to this love inhibits the manifestation of its union, whether this block takes the form of cold criticism, indifference, intolerance, or the feeling that "I am right and you are wrong."

These attitudes the practitioner must refrain from. He must see that everyone is struggling toward the light. He is one who is holding out a helping hand, gladly and willingly, feeling it the greatest privilege that can come to him. Out of his assurance that God is all there is, out of his knowledge that the Law of Mind in action will execute his word, he travels along the path of self-discovery for himself and others, sometimes blindly feeling his way, but always with an assurance that there is a way, a truth, and a life.

We should waste no time in futile arguments as to what religion or spiritual outlook is right or wrong, but gladly accept the evidence of anyone's prayer and faith as a demonstration of his belief. Too much time is lost in arguing whether or not one's philosophy is the only correct one, his religion the only true one, his method of procedure the only effective one. Let us leave these arguments to the contentions of smaller minds and try to find the thread of Truth running through all systems. Let us build on the affirmative and forget the negative.

Time spent in unprofitable argument is a waste of energy. Thousands of other persons have done what we are trying to do and without incorporating the particular ideas we employ. They have not said their prayers or made their affirmations in the same way, but if they have gotten a result they most certainly have used the same principle.

In this practice we learn to take everyone right where he is and build on the affirmative thoughts he already has. We should teach him to employ his faith in the most simple and direct manner possible to him. Gradually we can point out that his faith is built on the same principle we are using. In this way we more quickly gain cooperation, remove the differences of opinion produced by useless argument, and avoid a clash of ideas. We shall also be employing an attitude of non-resistance. We shall be seeing through the differences to the sameness.

In practical application, when a practitioner finds someone who is dogmatically opinionated, over-argumentative and resistant, instead of setting up a barrage of audible argument, he should silently treat to know that there is no resistance to the Truth. In this way he will be treating the resistance as he would any other negative state of consciousness.

In doing this there should be no sense of antagonism in the thought of the practitioner. He is seeing through the differences of opinion with the same clarity of thought that he uses in seeing through any other discord. Should his work stop or continue in the field of contentious argument, he will merely be accentuating the differences of opinion.

This calls for tolerance and love, sympathy and understanding. As a surgeon sets a broken bone with no personal opinion about his patient, seeking only to help him, so the spiritual mind practitioner readjusts thought with the same flexible tolerance and desire to be helpful.

A practitioner who argues with his patient is a poor practitioner. Unless he can resolve arguments through silent treatment, how is he going to get through to a place of acceptance? The scientific practitioner realizes that too much argument, of itself, is a part of the condition which needs to be changed.

The cold statement, "You are already perfect and the only thing wrong with you is your own false belief," will never heal. It will arouse antagonism and conflict, which will reflect back and forth, subconsciously, between the mind of the practitioner and the patient. The patient comes to the practitioner because he is sick or because he is going through some discordant or unhappy experience. He should be received in sympathy and with love, with tolerance and understanding, and never with a lofty attitude which looks down from the heights of its own conceit either in pity or condemnation. This attitude cannot heal.

Absolute sincerity is called for in spiritual mind treatment. No matter what he says audibly, the delicate mechanism of the mind will detect the slightest degree of insincerity. The practitioner must be sympathetic with a patient, even though he may not agree with his viewpoints. Just as he could not conscientiously criticize a patient because he has broken a limb, so he should not criticize him because of emotional disturbances. He is not setting himself up as a judge of human conduct. He is trying to help his patient to come to an inward sense of his own spiritual being, a realization of his own life rooted in pure Spirit.

The slightest sense of condemnation or judgment about the patient makes it impossible for his mind to receive the meaning of the truth audibly stated. No matter what the physical fact or its psychological cause which we seek to eradicate may be, if we stop merely in the physical effect or its mental cause we are falling short of spiritual realization, which alone can create a new mental cause and a new physical effect.

This cannot be done unless we rise above negative thought as well as physical inharmony. If we have the sincerity to believe and the scientific understanding to know that wherever there is the slightest negative thought about the patient in the mind of the practitioner it is bound to register in the treatment, then we shall understand the necessity of keeping our thoughts simple and direct, sincere and understanding at all times.

No mere series of statements, howsoever beautiful or spiritual in their implication, alone can do this. It calls for a deep and

112

penetrating sense of love, a sincere and direct approach to the Spirit in oneself and others. It also calls for great flexibility in dealing with oneself and others. It calls for patience and kindness, for sympathy and compassion—a sympathy with the person, but not with the wrong that assails him.

It calls for a complete clearance of the practitioner's thought about his patient. He must rise above the mistake and consequence to that place which exists at the center of everything, that which is original, pure and perfect. Unless one has a deep and sincere conviction that there is such a place, that such a reality actually exists, no words that he can use will uncover that perfection.

Spiritual mind practice is a combination of logic and reason, applied for the purpose of spiritual discernment. Through clear thinking one gradually penetrates to the Spirit. The logic, reasoning, affirmations, denials and statements used in a mental treatment are ways and methods for the conscious clearing of thought. Behind them must be a motivation of love, of sympathy and compassion—something which moves out from a deep, fundamental feeling about the Divine Presence.

After listening to negative statements from a patient the practitioner is the first one who has to be healed. The entire sense of lack, of evil and limitation, which the patient has described, must be repudiated in the mind of the practitioner. He silences the argument of fear, doubt and uncertainty in his own consciousness.

Another and equally important thing for a practitioner in this field to remember is that in order to expel a wrong consciousness from the mind of his patient he must first expel it from his own consciousness. It is in this sense that metaphysical healing becomes self-healing, as though the practitioner actually healed himself of the belief that assails his patient.

113

It is in this sense that the spiritual mind practitioner deals with his own consciousness and not with the consciousness of his patient. One mind is not manipulating another. The practitioner is not suggesting anything to his patient. He is actually removing a block which is interfering with the patient's self-expression. But he is removing it in his own awareness. He has no one to deal with but himself.

The practitioner persists in treatment until a definite objective change is brought about in the patient's experience. When this has happened the patient will want to know what is happening, and how. It is the duty of the practitioner, just as soon as possible, to put the patient on his own mental and spiritual feet, to show him how to work for himself.

No one is permanently healed in this science until he knows that he can consciously use the Law for himself, until he knows that he is rooted in pure Spirit and that his own word is the law of his own being. He is healed when he no longer needs help. Until this time he is merely relieved of a condition. When the time comes that he understands how conditions in his life flow out of his own consciousness and that he can change his consciousness—when this time arrives he is really healed. He need no longer depend upon a practitioner.

It is the duty of the practitioner to free his patient as soon as possible from the thought that he must lean on the practitioner. This is not only a duty, it is a privilege and produces a beneficent result in his own consciousness. In such degree as he has established a person in a conviction of spiritual freedom, he has likewise established himself in greater freedom than he ever had before.

This is why Jesus, who had such profound insight into the Law and into the Spirit, emphasized the thought that life gives to us as we give to others. That which is loosed is really held, that which is surrendered can be kept—"Who loses his life shall find it."

This concept is so high that our stumbling feet follow it with uncertainty, and yet, always with the assurance that he who has found God has discovered the pearl of great price. Spiritual pearls are created in the depths of consciousness and strung on the rosary of life, whose beads may be counted.

As the practitioner frees himself he is freeing his patient, and likewise, as he frees his patient he is freeing himself. The two freedoms go together because they are really one freedom. In spiritual mind practice we do not deal with many spirits, many minds or many bodies. We deal with one Spirit, one Mind, and one universal body—the body of right ideas whose prototype is hidden in the Spirit of God. Each individual is rooted in this universal Cause, projected by It, and held in place through Its law.

When the one suffering from physical illness has condemned the organs of his body by saying, "My poor head!" or, "My poor heart!" or, "My weak eyes!" etc., he should be taught to praise these organs into right action, to inwardly realize that they have an office to perform. What the Spirit has created cannot be a mistake. The mistake is in our viewpoint and never in the idea itself. Therefore, we seek to transpose our ideas.

For each wrong we seek to find its exact opposite, which will be the reality about that wrong. The truth about pain is peace, the truth about fear is faith, the truth about lack is abundance, the truth about hell is heaven, the truth about the devil is God.

The practitioner should give his patient the assurance that there is a divine beneficence in the universe, that love wishes to make the gift of life. He should help his patient to have a constructive faith in the universe, an optimistic outlook on life.

Frequently it is asked when the patient will be ready to

receive these great truths. He is ready when we are in a position to explain these truths to him, simply, sincerely and with deep conviction and feeling. He is ready on his first visit to a practitioner. Some power within him has drawn him to the practitioner for the purpose of having the truth revealed to him. This is what he has come for. When he walks through the door of the practitioner's office he is ready to receive all the practitioner has to give him, to understand all the practitioner has to tell him, to realize all the practitioner is able at that time to realize for him.

There is no conceit, no bigotry in this practice. There is no holier-than-thou attitude. It must be a thing of sincerity and simplicity. The practitioner who mistakenly believes that his patient is not ready to receive the great truths he has to offer, upon closer examination of his own consciousness will discover that he, himself, is not yet ready to deliver those truths. He can make real to his patient anything that is real to him, the reason being that the patient's spiritual status has never been touched by experience. Spiritually he is already where the practitioner is spiritually, and when deep calls unto deep, deep will answer deep. There will be a simultaneous agreement.

The practitioner loves the patient back to his own center. With technical knowledge of practice he removes the blocks which obstruct the passage of Spirit in the patient's experience. He does not establish the patient in Truth, in God or in Life. He merely takes him by the mental hand and leads him back into himself. His entire effort, whether it be audible explanation or silent practice, is to establish the patient in his own spiritual center.

Spiritual mind practice is a combination of mental technique and spiritual consciousness which establishes a faith and a conviction in the reality of good. The practitioner should never condemn his patient, or say, "You are suffering because you have done this or that or something else." Unless the practitioner can rise above both the mistake and its consequence, he will heal neither. He cannot rise above the mistake while he attaches it to his patient any more than he could rise above a mistake in his own personal life if he attaches it to his own spirit.

There can be no permanent healing without a spiritualization of consciousness. A permanent healing takes place in such degree as consciousness turns inward to the Source of being and finds itself united with life, with love, with God. This is what we call spiritual awareness and it is fundamental to all permanent healing.

The patient must be shown that he has personal and immediate access to all the presence and all the power there is in the universe. A practitioner's work is good only when he has grounded his patient firmly in a consciousness of his own personal contact with Reality. Always the practitioner is seeking to free the patient from the necessity of having a practitioner, from the belief that he must depend on anything but the Truth.

"Where the treasure is, there is the heart also." If one is led to believe that he must have a psychologist or a spiritual practitioner every time his thought is disturbed, he is still in bondage. The bondage may be a little sweeter, but it nevertheless springs from a poverty of thought. He will always be seeking external aid. This is good in temporary difficulty, but even this good could become an actual evil.

He must be taught that no other person could possibly possess anything which he does not already have. He should be taught that he is merely seeking a temporary aid. He should be grateful for such aid, but he should be shown that all discord arises from the belief that life is separated from the Spirit which lives in us.

No healing can be permanent, no series of treatments, no

matter how well-intentioned, is adequate unless the consciousness of the individual is awakened to the realization that the
individual life is God manifesting as that life. A practitioner
should never permit people to lean on him personally, other
than in a very temporary manner.

One of the problems that confronts a practitioner is how to
free his patient from the bondage of continually turning to
external aid, whether it be physical, mental or spiritual. First of
all, the practitioner must free himself from this bondage. He
must be certain that he does not place himself spiritually above
another, because in so doing he would be imposing bondage on
his own experience.

As the practitioner feels himself to be free in the Spirit he
must know that his patient has an equal freedom. He must definitely work to know that his patient is not bound by any person, condition or system of thought. In psychology this is called
"breaking the transference," which means putting wholeness
back into the patient, causing him to know that his own self-
awareness is sufficient.

This does not mean that he should be taught that he is alone
in the universe or that he need no longer companion with other
people. Quite the reverse. No person is spiritually whole who
seeks isolation from life. No person is spiritually whole who
feels that he can no longer mingle with people or participate in
human events. This would not be a healing. It would be a with-
drawal from life. The hermit who isolates himself from life that
he may be holy, is a sick person. It is only when we see God
everywhere and in everything and through all people that we
unify with life.

When this kind of healing takes place the individual automatically is adjusted to life. He can meet any problem that confronts him. A person who is spiritually healed will have a greater

zest in living than ever before; he will like people better. Tolerant of their mistakes, as he is with his own, he will learn to unite with that in them which is beyond littleness.

It is the business of a spiritual practitioner to so heal consciousness that this adjustment automatically takes place. This is what Jesus had in mind when he said that if we seek the Kingdom first, everything else will be added to it. If we find God in all men, we shall discover that all men are in God.